PRAISE FOR *THE FORGOTTEN ART OF BEING ORDINARY*

"Equally poetic and practical, this is a must-read for anyone whose job it is to navigate the role of media technology in our lives, which is all of us (parents, professionals, educators, etc.). It answers the questions we've all been asking and gets us to the future we all long for faster."

—Michelle Hord, former NBCUniversal Executive, Author, and Founder of Gabrielle's Wings.

"Filled with bangers guaranteed to change the way we perceive and comprehend the content vortex we live inside today, *The Forgotten Art of Being Ordinary* is a guidebook full of hope and reason, spirit and sound arguments."

—Andrew McLuhan, Director of The McLuhan Institute

"CJ has the rare ability to crystallize hunches that many of us have. In his thoughtful prose, we are given language to help us make sense of our chaotic era . . . as well as the optimism and hope to do something about it."

—Kim Lear, Multigenerational Researcher & Founder of Inlay Insights

"A remarkably thoughtful reflection on our use of media (and its use of us), CJ has created the soulful successor to Neil Postman's *Amusing Ourselves to Death* for the metaverse age. *The Forgotten Art of Being Ordinary* is a must-read."

—Jelani Memory, Founder & CEO of A Kids Co.

THE FORGOTTEN ART
OF BEING ORDINARY

Also by CJ Casciotta

*Get Weird: Discover the Surprising
Secret to Making a Difference*

THE FORGOTTEN ART OF BEING ORDINARY

A Human Manifesto in the
Age of the Metaverse

CJ CASCIOTTA

Matt Holt Books
An Imprint of BenBella Books, Inc.
Dallas, TX

Matt Holt is an imprint of BenBella Books, Inc.
10440 N. Central Expressway
Suite 800
Dallas, TX 75231
benbellabooks.com
Send feedback to feedback@benbellabooks.com.

BenBella and *Matt Holt* are federally registered trademarks.

Printed in the United States of America
10 9 8 7 6 5 4 3 2 1

Library of Congress Control Number: 2023002265
ISBN 9781637743171 (paper over board)
ISBN 9781637743188 (electronic)

Editing by Katie Dickman
Copyediting by James Fraleigh
Proofreading by Kellie Doherty and Lisa Story
Text design and composition by Aaron Edmiston
Cover design by Victor Huckabee
Printed by Lake Book Manufacturing

> **Special discounts for bulk sales are available.**
> **Please contact bulkorders@benbellabooks.com.**

FOR MACKINLEY,
A DOVE WITH CLAWS

CONTENTS

Technologies are like cannibals that eat alive
all existing populations. The first person
to get swallowed is the consumer. There's
nothing neutral about any technology.

—Marshall McLuhan in *Forbes* magazine
March 15, 1967

It's long been noted that "we become what we behold." When we create something new, we are in turn re-created. With every new technology comes a new human, a new human society. When we change who we are, we change what matters to us. Our values.

There was a time when technological change happened gradually enough to be barely noticeable except as a wistful reminiscence of the 'good old days' when things were simpler. Change happened slowly enough for humanity to adjust. As with every other creature on the planet, we relied on the slow and sure hand of evolution to do the heavy lifting.

Now, our technological environment shifts so drastically and quickly that any leisurely adjustment feels nearly impossible.

On the contrary, in recent centuries, the pace and scale of technology has sped up and grown so vast that we have whiplash from the metamorphosis. We're confused, dismayed, and dragged along in the wake of our own progress.

As our discomfort increases, so do our chances of doing something about our situation, because even though we know something's not right, we're too jostled to clearly discern what that something is.

We are, however, not helpless.

While it may be common to think that technological change is simply too big to be understood much less controlled, that isn't necessarily the case. The twenty-first century allows us more agency, more autonomy, and more capacity for understanding than we realize. It's not easy. But it *is* possible.

My grandfather, Marshall McLuhan, might have twenty-first-century citizens remember it's in the development stage that we arrange what will be the personal and social consequences of our innovations, but it isn't until the deployment stage that we pass the point of no return.

With more than two millennia of recorded hindsight as our guide, now more than ever we have the ability to anticipate not just the benefits but also much of the potential hazards of our innovations—we just need the will.

We can become much more intentional about how and why we develop and introduce technologies. To do that, we have to think differently about technologies, broadening our awareness and deepening our understanding. We need to be more concerned with what technologies might do with us than what we might do with them.

Here lies hope. Eventually, we know, we have to wake from our inertia and confront our challenges. There comes a point when we can't ignore them anymore. One of the great things about us humans has always been our ingenuity, our ability to solve any problem that comes our way. I firmly believe that we can figure this out, and it might be simpler than we think, more ordinary, as my friend CJ explains, than we've been strategizing. It might mean changing not just the ways we regard our technologies, but how we regard each other.

No, technology is not neutral, but neither are humans once they realize it.

Andrew McLuhan
Bloomfield, Ontario
2023

Volumes have been written on what media technology is doing to our individual and collective psyches. Social scientists, economists, technologists, and mental health experts all have contributed to this vast and crucial conversation. I hold none of these titles, a fact I admit intimidates me a bit when I consider you picking up this book and deciding whether or not to read it. I am, however, someone who makes a living creating media, trying my best to contribute words and pictures that improve our collective human journey in my own small way from my own little corner of the universe. I have done this very imperfectly, and at times I feel like media has gotten the best of me. Yet this is exactly why I am interested in exploring how we can use media technology wisely, rather than allow it to use us.

I'm also one of the very first digital immigrants, having grown up between the Gen X and millennial generations. I can remember swinging my fingers around our rotary phone. I can recall my family unboxing an America Online start-up CD-ROM and connecting us all to the wild, wild Web for the first time. My teenage years were spent enduring that annoying dialup sound, hoping it wouldn't wake my parents in the other room or rack their phone bill up too high. I distinctly remember watching the O. J. Simpson verdict live and the premiere of *American Idol* just a few years later, opening my first flip phone like I was Clint Eastwood dueling in some spaghetti Western, using my college email account to sign up for "the Facebook," and purchasing my first iPhone. I've witnessed what social psychologist Jonathan Haidt calls the progression of media's purpose from "connectivity" to "performance" firsthand, up close and personal. As someone who puts food on the table creating words and pictures, I am both exhilarated and haunted by the global unveiling of AI image generators and programs like ChatGPT during the final stages of writing this book. I wonder how exponentially different media technology will look by the time you read this.

Last, I'm a parent. I wrote most of this book between necessary doctors' appointments, requests for more Cheerios, and sprints to dance practice. I've often had to close my laptop in the middle of an introspective thought to address my kids' own urgent introspections: questions about the universe, their friendships, and whether a killer whale would beat a great white shark in a battle (spoiler: the whale always wins).

Like every parent, I've had to wrestle with the inevitable consequences that come with introducing media technology to our children—or withholding it. I've deliberated over how to raise healthy humans in an age of personal brands and algorithmic influencers under the dominion of an ever-branching metaverse*. . . all while wobbling around this new landscape myself.

I've allowed myself an extra pour on certain evenings over the past several years, after another troubling news story stopped us all dead in our tracks. I'll think about the world my kids will inherit; how the choices we make about what we value, and where we choose to direct our attention, will ultimately affect them.

I find myself devoting much of this thought to how we handle our tangled relationship with media, technology, and the metaverse, because I believe if we can get a grasp on that, a host of other problems will start to solve themselves.

The following pages are my humble attempt to form that grasp, to curl my fledgling fingers around a stubborn and twisted branch for the sake of any reader who, like me, finds themselves weary of a world that feels overrun by electronic devices and deprived of human connection.

---

*   There are varying points of view on what the term "metaverse" means. I give my own detailed definition in chapter two.

The answer has never been to go back to the Dark Ages. The answer is to unearth the renaissance. I've come to believe it's murmuring inside the bones of ordinary people like you and me.

BRANDING IS FOR COWS. BELONGING IS FOR PEOPLE.

OLD HAUNTS

Don't remember me in stone
Use any of me worthwhile to build your home upon
Don't bother wasting any wood
I'm already in every tree that will shade you
And don't bury me too deep
There's sure to be enough for you to shovel and shoulder

But perhaps think of me in the most normal corners of
  your day
Between the kitchen sink and the dishwasher
Next to the cup ring on the dresser
While you're managing the dust bunnies or going back for
  milk

Because those are the places where I often forgot where I
  was
And who you were
And what we had
  Which was everything

You are not a brand.

You are a strange amalgamation of dust and conscious-ness born into the world against all perceivable odds. To believe that you are a brand is to dissociate yourself from such reality and exchange it for the illusion of control. That dissociation—the disconnect between you and the clay beneath your feet—is the subject of this book.

The idea of dissociation is tempting, so tempting that people have built an empire out of offering it to us all under the guise of certainty. The metaverse may have a name now, but it's been fermenting under more primitive aliases for decades, such as "virtual reality," "augmented reality," and "reality television."

Reality itself, however—the kind that pulses through our connective tissues and feeds magnolias all in a day's work—can also be cold and harsh and immovable. To spend most of our time projecting and polishing a brand that feels tethered to us yet seemingly separate is to fool ourselves with a sense of control, no matter how fleeting the feeling may be. This tethered-but-separate feeling, mused upon by mystics and prophets throughout the ages as the battle between the true and false selves, has never been so perfectly on display, so acutely identifiable, as with the rise of the personal brand: a collection of distant, cloud-held zeros and ones standing in for the molecular masterpiece of ordinary flesh and bone.

Branding has, and always will be, about ownership, or at least the illusion of it. Many marketers will tell you that the meaning of the word "brand" has softened over the centuries, but in so representing it, they are simply being true to their job title. For more than four thousand years, branding has unequivocally been about declaring, "This is mine."

The word "brand" comes from *brandr* in Old Norse, an ancient Germanic language from which modern Scandinavian languages evolved, and referred to a piece of burning wood. In late Middle English *brandr* became a verb meaning "to mark with a hot iron, permanently."[1] What exactly were people marking? Cave paintings suggest that early humans branded their livestock as far back as the Stone Age, first with tar and later, around 2000 BC, with fire. Meditating on such a mental image for too long might cause even the most callous consumer to ponder going vegan. Modern depictions of the cattle-branding process induce similar empathy, showing at least two people forcibly restraining a calf while a third presses a burning iron into its flesh.

Branding has always been an imposing act, an effort to singe and sear one's identity onto another's. It's objectifying. I don't need to draw the historical line between Stone Age cattle and modern humanity for you. The world expanded and so did man's recognition of what he thought he could own, what he could scorch with his mark, thus establishing dominion. This led to enslaved people bearing scars on their skin and Jewish people with numbers etched into their wrists.

While the way we mark things is no longer so oppressive or genocidal, make no mistake: we're still caught up in an unending race for ownership and control. The commonplace branding associated with products, services, and the corporations that sell them would have you believe what's being branded *are* those products and services. In reality, the aim of those companies is to brand *you*. Shortly after World War II, with the advent of the household television set, the early antecedents of today's media-technology empires began figuring out ways to sell a story within a story, one about you—what you liked and what you didn't, how you saw yourself, and, more importantly, how you wanted others to see you. These companies realized that a well-constructed story could substitute convincingly for your identity. We'll discuss this in more detail later, but for now, it's important to understand that their logic here was simple: if these media companies could get you to tell a story about yourself that gave you a sense of control, it became fairly easy for them to use that same story to control *you*. Branding has never been about who you are but *whose* you are.

Now, advance the timeline to the dawn of the twenty-first century, an age when both television set and studio are attached to your person at all times (if you allow them the privilege). The notion that you yourself are a brand is simply another corporate tactic in the quest for ownership. Digital goods are cheaper to mass-produce than, say, soft drinks or dishwasher detergent. Even more advantageous is a recip-rocal business model that requires you to freely surrender your private, personal information in exchange for the illu-sion that you are in charge of what you see, hear, make, and share. Again, when they get you to tell a story you feel you can control, it's easier for them to control you with that story. It's like letting the cow decide where it wants to put its own-er's mark—a "colonization of the self" as one artist put it.[2]

If cave paintings are any indication, the inherent per-mission we feel to violently claim "I own this" and "This is mine" seems to rest deep in our collective psyche. Might this be the very root of our consumerism, the source of our indi-vidualistic thinking? Perhaps, but I'd argue there's a more ancient attribute, rooted even deeper inside us: humankind is deeply bent toward kinship, toward a physical and present belonging to living and natural things, toward an interde-pendence that seems to predate any act of ownership.

Equally present in those cave paintings is an undeniable sense of belonging. It's not hard to find etchings of people hunting and cooking together, protecting each other, sharing labors—the appearance of a social group designed to meet each other's needs and desires. While various forms of belonging can be found throughout the animal kingdom, it's practiced most mysteriously and intricately among our kind. For example, anthropologists have observed that while other animals largely rely on members of their immediate bloodline, humans throughout history have displayed a curious characteristic that they call "fictive" or "voluntary" kinship. In pursuing this uncommon kind of kinship, our belonging drive doesn't stop at blood, who we mate with, or even our own species, but ventures outside these boundaries to commune with any living thing that will accept us in our ordinary form—any being that won't attempt to own us or control us. This kind of reliance runs deeper than the "this is mine" mentality and instead declares, "this is ours."

I'm convinced that if we are to create any sustainable progress that allows us to thrive as a species past the twenty-first century, we must embrace the mentality that we first belong to the earth rather than believing it solely belongs to us. Reverence always proceeds a renaissance.

This book is an urgent call to rediscover that reverence, a reverence for all that is given and not manufactured, for all that grows wildly and unforced during a time in our history when we can flippantly swipe between natural and artificial. It's a book that begs us not to repeat the mistakes of history, to continue to evolve and not *de*volve, lest we deceive our-selves that such devolution equals progress.

A metaverse without reverence for the universe is a magic trick, a regression to a dark age marked by spells, impulse, and human sacrifice.

Artificial intelligence without reverence for organic intelligence is a cheap popcorn movie with the same damn ending we've seen over and over again.

Listen to the prophets, the poets, and the sci-fi story-tellers. You are not a brand. You are an ordinary human. So am I.

Just what does that mean exactly? For one thing, it means we're not alone. Second, it means we have a respon-sibility to do something about it.

02

BEARING
WITNESS

THE FORGOTTEN ART OF BEING ORDINARY

There was a woman who was relieved at your arrival
And a man whose name had a new meaning.
No one objected to you collapsing after your journey.
Your stillness was their stillness.

I think it's strange Christ was asked to perform miracles
As if the incarnation wasn't interesting enough—
The divine bed wetting, the sacrificial knee scrape,
The wobbly wooden chair.

But we often prefer a spectacle, something to show for all
    the suffering,
A little magic we can manufacture.

So we sear our names into the asphalt,
Scratch our legacies in digital dust.

The soil, however, holds your history.
The river sees herself in you.
There are secrets about you only old trees know.

Hand yourself over to all the wild graces.
Dig your heels into your inheritance.
Put the earth back in you.
Practice the forgotten art of being ordinary.

In an age when you can be anything you want, why would anyone choose to be ordinary? After all, the twenty-first century is the age of the metaverse. While that's a vague buzzword with many definitions, I mean the rapidly expanding media landscape we humans inhabit, an umbrella term for the "second world" we occupy online where digital expressions of ourselves stand in for our ordinary flesh and blood. To me, any innovation labeled as the metaverse is simply the next iteration of a world we've been collectively building for a long while.

The metaverse invites us to build and brand whatever identity we desire and cast it like a shadow onto its walls. Our physical bodies remain the same, but in the metaverse we can make those shadows bigger and more encompassing so that our ordinary selves pale in comparison.

By contrast, to be ordinary is to realize the magnificent potential of such shadow casting and instead draw the shades wide open on ourselves, causing the very things others may require or expect us to magnify to shrink under the influence of such blanketing light. It's a conscious effort to look at the limitations of our own flesh and blood with the same kindness and generosity we offer our most curated and idealized projections.

This practice isn't a lessening of one's self but a return to it. If it weakens anything, it takes power away from our meta-projections and redistributes it back into the hands that carry the blessing of being able to feel dirt and wind and another's skin.

Such a practice, an art form really, has become all but antithetical in this era of personal brands and pixelated curtains. We've not been told enough that our dignity begins and ends with our physical existence, that we aren't just meat membranes in service to digital copies. Absent this advice, we end up not seeing each other anymore; instead we engage each other's media. That one degree of separation is important, especially when many of us go about our day unconscious of the fact that it even exists.

And here is where the greatest challenge lies. To be ordinary is not to be curmudgeonly. To move around with a sense of cynicism about the state of it all, to tell the twenty-first century to "get off my lawn"—an attitude of which I've often found myself guilty—is, in reality, its own kind of self-infatuation. It falsely excuses us from having to engage the era in which we find ourselves and isolates us from a culture that will continue to advance technologically whether we participate or not. This detached attitude still finds us whittling away, creating our own kind of personal brand: a projection of superiority and ambivalence, one that points a finger rather than lends a hand.

What, then, does it mean to be ordinary, if it's not being a relic or a hermit or, for that matter, someone who welcomes this ever-intensifying media-verse without a thought of concern or reflection?

The forgotten art of being ordinary is also the art of bearing witness to something other than ourselves. It's the practice of telling each other's story instead of following the impulse to broadcast our own. It's leveraging the technology afforded to us not to construct a more perfect version of ourselves, but rather to reconstruct the untold and fragmented narratives of those with whom we find ourselves in uncompromised communion.

Growing up in a fundamentalist environment, I learned to fear humility. The thought of "being humbled" by God, being made a fool because of any mismanaged pride, robbed like Job of anything good just to teach me a lesson, was enough to keep an already neurotic twelve-year-old up at night.

I had no idea humility could feel so much like freedom, that its Greek root was the word *praus*, or power under control. I had no notion that the blessed removal of a thousand fig leaves could end in the confidence one only carries when one no longer needs to carry anything else.

To be ordinary, to be humble, is to be assured of your own completion without the need for any augmentation, any additional branding or meta-version, which as we know defies conventional corporate thinking and threatens the well-worn tactics of many media technology gatekeepers.

So, the task in front of us is large: to redefine how we choose to arrive at the shores of the metaverse, to handle the powerful chemical reaction of media and technology with more care than what's expected, protesting where it harms us and reimagining its potential to point us back to the beauty and abundance that lie in our ordinary, in-real-life selves.

It would be irrelevant if not vain to fill the pages of this book solely with warnings of the dangers of modern media we've mistakenly labeled as "social." By now most of us have heard about and experienced its addictive nature and corrosive consequences. What I will say is this. Just as twentieth-century citizens found themselves living through the Great Depression, today, in the twenty-first century, we are living through another crisis: the Great Distraction. We have every technological benefit at our fingertips, and we're using them primarily to uncouple ourselves from the native souls we incarnate until the gift of our consciousness is made homeless.

Therefore, I refuse to accept the frequent response that we cannot harness or control what seems all-consuming, that those consequences are somehow out of our power, that the boundaries of the metaverse cannot be re-identified, recategorized, and put in their proper place. We ordinary humans are more resilient than that.

So, for all our acknowledgment of the problems and challenges surrounding this conundrum, rather than continuing to shout "Get off my lawn!" I'd like us to spend our time together attempting to carve out some streams, form some handholds, and mold together the solutions within our grasp to the crisis of communication in which we find ourselves.

One of my favorite long-standing documents for guiding how humanity should act toward each other and their environment is the paradoxical collection of blessings from Christ's Sermon on the Mount known as the Beatitudes, or supreme blessings designed to kindle happiness. To cite two examples:

> "Blessed are the meek, for they shall inherit the earth."

> "Blessed are the merciful, for they shall receive mercy."[1]

The list goes on to eight to nine total, depending on how you interpret them. In the forthcoming chapters, I'll lay out what I'm facetiously dubbing "The Beatitudes of Media Technology," nine ruminations perhaps we can incarnate to recalibrate the way we communicate with each other. Call it my Sermon from a Keyboard.

It's my hope that you'll take to heart any of these ideas that resonate, begin to wrestle with their implications, and start to echo them in the spaces where advocacy, change, and reconciliation are most urgently needed. Some will take a courageous discomfort and a relentless patience, the weaponry of ordinary people throughout history.

Our coexistence with the widening metaverse has approached an apex where it is both completely fractured and all-consuming. Yet, we minimize that dissonance we feel at our own risk. Yes, the sun is still shining. Yes, we choose not to give into cynicism. But ordinary humans are too important, too miraculous to risk extinction. Our lack of reverence for our digital climate is just as great a threat to our species as our lack of regard for our physical one. And just like changing climate, there is hope yet. There are reverse courses we can take. There are solutions worthy of our collective time and effort. But they are not evergreen. Time is running out. Ordinary humans are endangered, but we're not gone yet.

03

THE GHOST OF JOHN HILL

Media as a Crisis Discipline

THEN THEIR EYES WERE OPEN

Adam slunk back on a mansion of wildflowers
While Eve tucked her neck into the soft spot beneath his
  chest.

"Wouldn't you like to know it all one day?
Good and evil, genesis, and revelation?"

"That sounds overwhelming," Eve whispered to Adam.
His mouth curled. "It sounds like God."

The question came from a small limbless body
Slim and sleek, almost metallic.

For centuries the Serpent waited and wondered if we'd
  ever get the punchline,
The picture of an apple with a bite taken out of it.

Beatitude

01.

BLESSED ARE THOSE WHO CONSIDER HUMANITY'S RELATIONSHIP WITH MEDIA AS URGENT A CRISIS AS ITS RELATIONSHIP TO CLIMATE, FOR THEY SHALL CORRECT OUR FATAL COURSE.

On a cold New York morning in 1953, John Hill was scribbling something on a legal pad while one of the executives who had flown in for the meeting droned on and on about the mountain they were up against. John was already busy working the various angles, paying little attention to the margins of his page. His straight, thinning, slicked-back hair and wire-rimmed glasses were unevenly cloaked by syncopated puffs of cigarette smoke circling around the long oval conference table.

A few weeks earlier, the CEOs of the three major tobacco companies had decided to meet at a secret location in New York City to discuss the fallout from recently released studies that directly linked cigarettes to cancer. Forget competition for the time being. This was a bombshell that affected all of them equally. For the first time since the Great Depression, sales were plummeting.

While many of their employees were busy buying last-minute Christmas gifts and stocking up on party essentials despite this year's meager bonuses, the men sat around John Hill's conference room, their cigarettes doing the heavy lifting of curbing their anxiety, helping them appear calm, collected, and in control.

John didn't wait for the droning voice to finish. After all, he was the president of the successful public relations firm that bore his name, and the CEOs had sought his advice. Time was of the essence and John never liked to waste it.

"Gentlemen, it seems you have two choices in front of you: deny the facts outright and risk being seen as acting merely out of your own self-interest, *or* simply drop a little doubt in the consumer's mind."

John understood the subtle difference between denying the facts and creating what Kellyanne Conway, the former presidential counselor to Donald Trump, once admitted are "alternative facts." In collaboration with John Hill's spin firm, the CEOs would hire their *own* scientists and researchers, who would portray the health effects of smoking as less conclusive than what "other" scientists and researchers would have you think.[1] The companies then crafted "A Frank Statement to Cigarette Smokers" and published it in about 450 newspapers in January of 1954.

The puff piece was littered with such bold assurances as "We accept an interest in people's health as a basic responsibility, paramount to every other consideration in our business" and "We always have and always will cooperate closely with those whose task it is to safeguard the public's health." As biotech researchers Kelly D. Browneell and Kenneth E. Warner later wrote in a study,

> The "Frank Statement" was a charade, the first step in a concerted, half-century-long campaign to mislead Americans about the catastrophic effects of smoking and to avoid public policy that might damage sales. Unearthed later, industry documents showed the repeated duplicity of its executives. Everything was at stake. The industry wanted desperately to prevent, or at least delay, shifts in public opinion that would permit a barrage of legislative, regulatory, and legal actions that would erode sales and profits.[2]

If that strategy carries an air of familiarity, it might be because it's become the method of choice for stalling multiple cultural crises of profound economic consequence. The rhetoric, "Of course we're concerned, but let's wait until we have *all* the data," has been used to impede reforms as varied as climate change and NFL concussion protocols. Now, it's become the morning song of media tech giants in response to external and even internal reports that something, to put it mildly, isn't quite right. Consider a report that came directly from the US Surgeon General in 2021:

From 2009 to 2019, the proportion of high school students reporting persistent feelings of sadness or hopelessness increased by 40%; the share seriously considering attempting suicide increased by 36%; and the share creating a suicide plan increased by 44%.

There is a clear need to better understand the impact of technologies such as social media on different kinds of users, and to address the harms to users most at risk.[3]

Marry that analysis with what former Facebook employee and data scientist Frances Haugen announced publicly that same year when she decided to blow a whistle on some of the company's more alarming practices:

Facebook's own research says it is not just that Instagram is dangerous for teenagers, that it harms teenagers, it's that it is distinctly worse than other forms of social media.

And what's super tragic is Facebook's own research says, as these young women begin to consume this—this eating disorder content, they get more and more depressed. And it actually makes them use the app more. And so, they end up in this feedback cycle where they hate their bodies more and more.

As you're well aware by now, the harmful effects of social media are not limited to teenagers or one specific gender. Haugen continued:

> So, you know, you have your phone. You might see only 100 pieces of content if you sit and scroll on for, you know, five minutes. But Facebook has thousands of options it could show you. The algorithm picks from those options based on the kind of content you've engaged with the most in the past. And one of the consequences of how Facebook is picking out that content today is it is—optimizing for content that gets engagement, or reaction. But its own research is showing that content that is hateful, that is divisive, that is polarizing, it's easier to inspire people to anger than it is to other emotions.[4]

But that's just one national study backed up by one insider. Besides, one could argue that perhaps Haugen was simply a disgruntled employee bending the facts to pursue some self-serving ulterior motive. Yet, three years earlier, in 2017, Chamath Palihapitiya, venture capitalist and Facebook's former vice president of user growth, who had been with the company since its early stages, had this to say:

> I think we all knew in the back of our minds, even though we feigned this whole line of

"unintended consequences," I think in the back recesses of our minds, something bad could happen. It literally is at a point now [where] we've created tools that are ripping apart the social fabric of how society works. That is literally where we are. I would encourage all of you to internalize this—if you feed the beast, the beast will destroy you.[5]

Palihapitiya went on to say that he doesn't let his children engage in any screentime whatsoever—a decision we may consider extreme, but then again, few of us can say we've carried his degree of influence on the creation and marketing of these products.

Let's revisit Haugen's revelations. As part of her whistle-blowing report, the ex-employee copied tens of thousands of internal company documents. One admission stands out in particular: "We have evidence from a variety of sources that hate speech, divisive political speech and misinformation on Facebook and the family of apps are affecting societies around the world."[6]

With such a sweeping indictment, the pressure on Facebook to respond was overwhelming. Did the giant media technology company, in a moment of courage and clarity, decide to diverge from John Hill's advice from fifty years earlier to question the research? I think you can guess. In a written statement to *60 Minutes* in response to Haugen's claims, a Facebook representative remarked:

Every day our teams have to balance protecting the right of billions of people to express themselves openly with the need to keep our platform a safe and positive place. We continue to make significant improvements to tackle the spread of misinformation and harmful content. To suggest we encourage bad content and do nothing is just not true. If any research had identified an exact solution to these complex challenges, the tech industry, governments, and society would have solved them a long time ago.

The response to inconvenient findings is always the harmonizing call that the data is conclusive—whether it's Big Media Tech responding to societal breakdown, Big Energy responding to climate consequences, Big Tobacco responding to cancer, or the NFL responding to concussion data.

It may seem simple, but it's worth concluding here: speculation should not be cause for inaction; inaction should be cause for speculation. That shift alone, executed by ordinary people and their representatives alike, would accelerate change on a global scale.

There's one significant difference between the problems of Big Tobacco and Big Media Tech: media technology's influence is all-encompassing. Yes, smoking was a cultural norm that turned into a health crisis, but with media technology, we are dealing with the underlying fabric of how we communicate with our fellow species, at both the micro and macro levels. This issue drastically influences almost every imaginable facet of society. It's economic, technological, informational, and political in nature. It's the conduit by which ideas and information travel and trade. If media technology fails us, everything fails us.

Unfortunately, the American government, which has nurtured Big Media Tech giants from humble saplings, seems to be miles behind the eight ball when it comes to recognizing the severity of this problem.

Perhaps what many members of government don't fully comprehend is that when it comes to media technology, our society-wide problem of polarization and misinformation is actually the same problem we are seeing unfold in our young people's mental health. We are spending most of our time using platforms specifically designed not only to alter our emotions, but temporarily reward us in a calculated Pavlovian way when those emotions are altered. Normally this would be neither a tragedy nor novel. Alcohol performs this same function, as do nicotine and other legal drugs. But we haven't labeled media technology platforms that knowingly produce these side effects as drugs. Instead, they're simply considered our news and information, our work, our play, our commerce, our discourse, our perception of the world and others. In our minds, they *are* us. We post, therefore we are. It's a stupefaction on a massive scale—the Great Distraction.

> The effect of electric technology had at first been anxiety. Now it appears to create boredom. We

THE GHOST OF JOHN HILL

have been through the three stages of alarm, resistance, and exhaustion that occur in every disease or stress of life, whether individual or collective.[7]

Media scholar Marshall McLuhan wrote that in 1964 about the media of his time, but the endless juxtapositions between anxiety and numbness, alarm and exhaustion, as advances in media have mercilessly barreled forward, have left us all the more reason to choose boredom and exhaustion as our default state. To reform this spiral—and to counter that exhaustion and boredom—will require us to fight the neurological limitations of our humanity.

Why? Because the state of media is a crisis, one that must be escalated to the level of climate change or global pandemics. Just as we let industrialism go unchecked since its revolution nearly two centuries ago and are now dealing with the urgent repercussions, we have sleepily allowed the internet—the most consequential, humanity-altering medium since the printing press—to be developed and distributed almost exclusively by the private sector without virtually any oversight or understanding.

In case you're thinking that this is beginning to sound like a "get off my lawn" rant from someone who wishes we could simply go back to the good ol' days of the twentieth century, hear me out. I'm not talking about the remarkable stockpile of good that media technology has afforded us. We could fill libraries of examples! How would the entire world have been made aware of George Floyd's murder had not a young woman recorded the entire ordeal on her phone's camera and uploaded it for the global population to see? What about those shedding a light on Vladimir Putin's unpopular invasion of Ukraine from within Russia? Consider the speed at which news of the suspicious death of twenty-two-year-old Mahsa Amini circulated after she was apprehended in 2022 by Iran's "morality police" for wearing clothes deemed inappropriate, and how quickly protesters were able to activate and rise up against an oppressive government. Better media technology shines a brighter light on injustice, making it harder for those who perpetuate flawed systems to hide.

And imagine living through the COVID-19 pandemic without media technology! Not only did the technological advances of the twenty-first century create new businesses and infrastructure, they sustained them! Media technology made it possible to update citizens with case counts and scientific breakthroughs in real time, allowing them to schedule immunizations from their smartphones. It afforded many the privilege of working from home or starting a business with nothing more than a computer and Wi-Fi connection. Perhaps most importantly, media technology also allowed friends and loved ones to retain some semblance of sensory connection to each other when ordinary physical contact was impossible.

When media technology enriches our ordinary lives, when it makes the touchable world brighter and bolder than a million pixels ever could, when it presses us toward an embrace of another, it is a gift, perhaps one of the most profound, to ordinary humans living in the twenty-first century.

What I am desiring for us in this moment is a greater sense of ownership of such a gift, to deny the proclivity to simply accept the overreach of bad-faith actors as a necessary evil, unfortunate side effects of an otherwise healthy advancement. I don't believe we need to settle for the sentiment that says we have to put up with the bad along with the good. If we do, I believe we're at risk of the former eclipsing the latter.

So, don't get off my lawn. Run freely all over it. Tear down its fences. But take notice of its flowers, be kind to them, water them if you can, and maybe pluck a weed that's choking one when you happen upon it.

It bears repeating: we must treat our burgeoning meta-climate with the same degree of care that we ought to be giving our physical one. And much like caring for our physical climate, the first step is accepting that it is indeed in crisis.

In 2021, a group of seventeen researchers from a swath of disciplines as varied as biology and philosophy published a paper arguing that the study of media technology's negative side effects should be raised to the level of a "crisis discipline":

> In addition to existential ecological and climatic threats, human social dynamics present

other challenges to individual and collective wellbeing, such as vaccine refusal, election tampering, disease, violent extremism, famine, racism, and war.

In response, regulators and the public have doubled down on calls for reforming our social media ecosystem, with demands ranging from increased transparency and user controls to legal liability and public ownership. The basic debate is an ancient one: Are large-scale behavioral processes self-sustaining and self-correcting, or do they require active management and guidance to promote sustainable and equitable wellbeing?

The situation parallels challenges faced in conservation biology and climate science, where insufficiently regulated industries optimize profits while undermining the stability of ecological and earth systems. Such behavior created a need for urgent evidence-based policy in the absence of a complete understanding of the systems' underlying dynamics.[8]

Common sense would say that it will be a combination of self-correction and active guidance that steers the metaverse in the direction we ordinary people imagine and hope for. You and I carry a hope-filled agency unshackled to boards and bureaus. We don't need to wait for more studies to be conducted to *ensure* without the shadow of a doubt that we are indeed staring at a point of no return, where the smog envelops the sun. We can contribute to both the self-correction and the overarching guidance. We can act where powerful people are prone to stall. We can choose which platforms we use and how we use them. We can teach our children to do the same. We can vote for those who understand the significance of this crisis, leaders who will practice the forgotten art of being ordinary, shaping the metaverse to serve the good of the people instead of their personal brand. We can't put the genie back in the bottle, but we can help form the future we imagine with our own hands.

Our work can start by recognizing three urgent "perception shifts" and doing whatever we can within our own agency to teach, advocate, and embody them, becoming squeaky wheels among a landfill of passive pixels.

First, we must change what we talk about when we talk about media literacy.

Andrew McLuhan, the grandson of Marshall McLuhan, is the director of the McLuhan Institute, which was created to carry on Marshall's work of exploring and understanding culture and technology. He notes the difference between the kind of conventional media literacy being taught to kids today and what he calls "macro-media literacy." Conventional media literacy is largely concerned with the content each type of media is sending and how to critically discern it, create it, and share it with others. While this is good, necessary work, it's not the full picture. It still mistakenly separates the medium from the message, the opposite of what Andrew's grandfather spent much of his life arguing against. As Andrew writes,

> While people are busy making content—even when they're busy "being critical" of content, technologies are quite busy rearranging our senses, our brains, and our societies. And they do this regardless of "the message" you're critically or uncritically occupied with.[9]

In other words, it's one thing to teach the next generation how to use these existing platforms as ethically and healthily as possible, but if they do not understand that some platforms are inherently built to be more divisive than others, if they're not taught that a cigarette inherently contains nicotine, how much good can that really accomplish? McLuhan continues:

> Macro media literacy analyzes the effect of technologies, regardless of their content, on humans. It focuses on the wider "psychic and social consequences," on the cognitive and neurological effects, the reshaping of our senses and the balance among them, and the very "wiring" of our brains. It is in this manipulation that we see the major changes in people individually and collectively.[10]

I'm not suggesting that we ought to go around teaching children that all media platforms are inherently immoral. That would be counterproductive. Focusing on their effects and not simply their content, however, would be one of the first steps in helping people start contextualizing media technology for what it is, distinguishing between natural, ordinary reality and something one artificially constructs or extends. Then, and only then, would they begin to disentangle and "disembody" from it, distinguishing themselves from the shadows it allows them to project and learning to make critical choices about what they decide to give their attention to and what they don't.

Second, we must reset media technology's purpose from performance back to connection.

If you think about it, there are very few models for healthy human interaction that currently exist in our twenty-first-century media landscape. Look at the loudmouthed snarky pundit format or split screen personalities talking over each other in a desperate duel to say the most words. Social media is no exception. In his piece for the *Atlantic*, titled "Why the Past 10 Years of American Life Have Been Uniquely Stupid," social scientist Jonathan Haidt breaks down the moment social media shifted from a method meant to connect people to a method that rewarded performance:

> In their early incarnations, platforms such as Myspace and Facebook were relatively harmless. They allowed users to create pages on which

to post photos, family updates, and links to the mostly static pages of their friends and favorite bands.

But gradually, social-media users became more comfortable sharing intimate details of their lives with strangers and corporations . . . they became more adept at putting on performances and managing their personal brand—activities that might impress others but that do not deepen friendships in the way that a private phone conversation will.

It was around this time, circa 2009 (when Palihapitiya would have been steeped in his executive role), that Facebook and Twitter began to introduce tools designed to evoke validation and promote virality, buttons with seemingly innocuous names like "like" and "share." Haidt continues:

Once social-media platforms had trained users to spend more time performing and less time connecting, the stage was set for the major transformation, which began in 2009: the intensification of viral dynamics.

The ability to slow down or dampen that intensification so that the purpose of media technology operates more as a utility for connection than a product for performance would be a helpful step in the right direction.

Frances Haugen, the Facebook whistleblower I mentioned earlier, also advocates for this kind of dampening in a way that feels reasonable and achievable rather than sweeping, damning, and therefore unrealistic. In an interview with NPR she explained how her aim is not censorship but for simple algorithmic changes to platforms such as Facebook:

> If a reshare chain gets more than, say, two hops long, you [should] have to take a moment and copy and paste. No one is stopping you. You really want to keep spreading that idea? Copy and paste. Let's not knee-jerk that...That friction, having a chance to take that extra breath, actually reduces the amount of toxic content that gets spread.[11]

Perhaps the deliberate decision to go slower—not because we are technically incapable of it, but because we are *psychologically* and *sociologically* incompatible with the devices we have created, because going faster would stand in direct opposition to the gift of our ordinariness—is not an admission of failure but a sign of wisdom. It's one that's age-old, a proverb sci-fi prophets like Mary Shelley and Robert Louis Stevenson smuggled into their cautionary tales, stories of men creating and becoming monsters.

Limitation is the enemy of the foolish, but it's Eden for the ordinary, those who know they can create whatever reality they want, but also know that doing so means abandoning the only one that's irreplaceable.

Last, and perhaps most consequential, we must realize media technology has become the next inequity issue.

As I write this in the year 2022, it seems like every week another young celebrity is choosing to opt out of all social media. Today it's Tom Holland, the young, in-demand Spider-Man. Last week, *Stranger Things* star Millie Bobby Brown opened up about her breakup with social media, how she's in therapy for cyberbullying, and how others now maintain her accounts. Before that, pop sensation Selena Gomez announced she hasn't personally been on social media for the past several years, yet still has a "brand presence," a direct result of her success as a celebrity.

The option to "unplug" from the online world, to raise children without screentime, to work and play without being tethered to a device, will increasingly become a luxury granted only to the few. Ask the single mother of three living on minimum wage in a high-crime neighborhood whether she has the margin to monitor her kids' screentime and she might laugh at you. Any parent who's tried keeping their kid from falling victim to the Great Distraction understands the amount of time, intentionality, and commitment it takes, not to mention the fact that "unplugging" becomes a whole lot easier when one can afford to offer kids alternatives dazzling enough to distract them (e.g., Disney World is a better experience than Disney+, but one that comes with a much higher barrier to entry).

In his book *Average Is Over,* economist Tyler Cowen predicts that those who can't afford the educational luxuries of the rich such as private tutoring will resort to less personal (but more scalable) online learning content as a more affordable option. In other words, the less money you make, the more dependent you'll be on media technology. Not only that, but as some of these celebrity announcements suggest, a new kind of servitude will begin to emerge, the role of the "digital servant" offered to wealthy elite who can afford to take a hands-off approach. While the upper class may be able to afford mental health services for their flirtations with social media, the odds that their servants will be able to access such help seem slim given how expensive and inaccessible mental health care now is. More worrisome, if we already know that media technology creates an unhealthy cognitive dissonance between our physical selves and our disembodied digital shadows, how much more dissonance could that create for digital servants when twice removed?

Left unchecked, it will surely be seen as the next iteration of systemic discrimination, tuned to the same key as Jim Crow, redlining, and the war on drugs.

However inconvenient this might sound, the option to live free and independent from the Great Distraction is, in fact, a civil rights issue. Once we see it as such, we can begin to think practically about making that option possible for everyone.

Approaching the ways we handle media technology (and the ways it handles us) with a sense of severity, urgency, and public responsibility is different from simply choosing to shut it off, disengage from its influence, and go about our day unaffected by the looming crisis outside our window. That's a choice made from privilege and self-protection. The forgotten art of being ordinary is a sacred recognition that in a world of selfies, we belong to a tribe, that our individual actions (and inactions) ripple through a greater collective. If that's true, we must lay down our individual digital dynasties, for the sake of a collective one. We must teach the whole story of media's impact from a fuller understanding, use that knowledge to ward off its more harmful tendencies, and advocate for reforms that work for everyone, rather than simply allowing the privileged few to completely dodge its challenges.

Once we assess the damage, acknowledge the crisis for what it is, count our living, and hold them with a new kindness, we can start to pick up the pieces and build a sturdier bridge to the future. Seeing the nightmare for what it is, we can inoculate against its ability to haunt us. More importantly, we can start to compose a better dream.

04

THE REVOLUTION WILL NOT BE STREAMED

Media and the American Dream

TO HAVE AND TO HOLD

pockets packed

with wind

full tank and

sleepy eyes

I nod to the sunrise like we're about to race

down the interstate

past wild pines

like Steinbeck

like Kerouac

like Simon

I'll crawl across

this country

this molecular experiment

married to me

oil and vinegar

black and white

blood and salt water

here's what I want

to trace my fingers across

its curves and valleys

flesh tones and flashes of neon

to smell sweat

on a freshly picked banjo

echoes of ancestors

who picked heavier things

to stroll past porches
and stoops
and awnings
sinner sanctuaries
graced with cricket choirs

stop to taste the holy water
made by a neighbor
the gifts of God
for the people of God

let me listen with my mouth
read with my toes
press my prints against
clay and concrete
stories and riddles
now old enough to rhyme

all this time
my wife
sits over in the corner
giving me her
permissive eyes
and I've been staring at my phone.

Beatitude

02.

BLESSED ARE THOSE WHO LONG FOR A FIREPLACE MORE THAN A JETPACK, FOR THEY SHALL REVITALIZE THE AMERICAN DREAM.

What does our pursuit of happiness currently look like in the age of the metaverse? Is it achievable? To what end?

> It's deep in the race for a man to want his own
> roof and walls and fireplace.

That line from the classic Frank Capra film *It's a Wonderful Life* (one of my favorite movies, as I know it is for many) was the pervading sentiment regarding the American Dream in 1946—a year after World War II had ended. Capra, an Italian immigrant, much like my own Italian grandmother, made passage to America with his family at the age of five via the steerage compartment of a steamship, the cheapest and arguably most miserable way to travel.

Pulling into New York Harbor, Capra remembered his father pointing toward the Statue of Liberty and exclaiming, "Look at that! That's the greatest light since the star of Bethlehem! That's the light of freedom! Remember that."

Capra grew up in what he described as "the Italian Ghetto" of Los Angeles. He fought in World War I, hopped freight trains across the Western frontier in his twenties, and became one of the most influential media minds of twentieth-century American cinema.[1] It's fair to say Frank Capra felt a kinship with the American Dream.

It's a Wonderful Life is full of "Caprisms" like the line about roofs and walls and fireplaces. I'm not saying they're not idealistic; they were, even for their time. But to Capra, ideals were everything. And it's worth focusing on what ideals he considered American and what weren't—the latter being manifested in the film's villain, Mr. Potter, the ruthless real-estate banker. Potter, admittedly without much character development or backstory, represents an unchecked overreach of a certain kind of capitalism responsible for the destruction of that American Dream. To Capra, the unrelenting capitalist who put profit over people wasn't widely regarded as something to be achieved or attained and certainly not something to be rewarded. (Side note: the FBI did circulate a memo claiming the film attempted to discredit bankers by casting one as a villain, claiming it "maligned the upper class," a tactic they believe smelled like Communist propaganda.[2]) In reality, Capra, a card-carrying Republican, created an archetype in Potter that represented an ever-lurking lust and avarice for excess and control that has always threatened the common good. Potterism has always been with us, predating the character himself. Capra even contrasts his villain's character with that of the generous capitalist Sam Wainwright, who, due to his industrious investment in converting soybeans into plastic, is ultimately able to wire George the money he needs at the end of the film.[3]

Perhaps it takes an immigrant mindset, one well acquainted with memories of true scarcity and voyages across violent seas, to help the rest of us understand just how indefensible and destructive Potterism is.

Compare that sentiment with that of today's industrial icons like Jeff Bezos, Mark Zuckerberg, and Elon Musk, an immigrant privileged from birth. There is an overarching belief that these entrepreneurs have successfully achieved the twenty-first-century version of the American Dream, becoming the new gold standard in what it means to have accomplished greatness. Somewhere in between black-and-white and ultra-high-definition TV, the American idea of happiness has managed to shift drastically from attaining a roof, some walls, and a fireplace to owning a private jet, multiple homes, a billion-dollar bank account, and a sense that those things should be achieved at all costs, without a guiding spirit of balance or consideration for the means by which they are achieved.

Alternatively, the forgotten art of being ordinary means to behold with reverence all that we've been given, to comprehend the touchable grace that heaves in the marriage of molecules every single day without us sanctioning them, to see the "enoughness" of every thing.

Enoughness, the antithesis of Potterism, is at odds with the allure of the metaverse, which many a big media company has eagerly exploited. Rather than regard and nurture the earth's finite resources, we find it easier than ever to turn our attention to building infinite imaginary worlds. When reality feels painfully inadequate, we can instead nurse that pain by simulating the ideal. Online, a healthy sense of ambition is easily replaced by mimetic desire. If we can't have what Bezos has, the right curation tools and filters can at least make it seem like we do. Our FOMO is quickly patched with faux-mo. Instead of a more content culture, the result is a culture that simply produces more content.

The problem of most people no longer being able to achieve the American Dream—evolving as it has to include owning a super-yacht or jetpack—can't be fixed by simply allowing them to own those things in the metaverse. Similarly, the solution to pricing the masses out of a trip to Disney World can't be to offer them a streaming service. We cannot keep sticking screens in front of people as the primary solution to the growing chasm of inequality they face. That's a recipe for a unique kind of uprising: not a traditional one full of violence and action, but a passive revolt, one of satiated apathy and petrified will. People will destroy by refusing to create, spread chaos by refusing to get their fingers dirty.

Take Japan, for example.

You may think it's weird to talk about Japan when discussing the state of the American Dream, but from my vantage point, since World War II, Japan has acted as an accelerated micro-version of America, experiencing many of the economic and cultural triumphs and destabilizers we have in double and triple time, often shortly before we do. If you want to understand where America is heading culturally and technologically, look at what's happening in Japan now.

Since the beginning of the twenty-first century, Japan has been wrestling with what looks like a surface-level cultural phenomenon whose cause nonetheless has deeper implications: Japan has found itself heavily populated with males who claim to be voluntarily celibate, a demographic known as "herbivore men."

A 2013 *Guardian* interview with Ai Aoyama, a Japanese sex and relationship counselor, explains:

> Japan's under-40s appear to be losing interest
> in conventional relationships. Millions aren't
> even dating, and increasing numbers can't
> be bothered with sex. For their government,
> "celibacy syndrome" is part of a looming national
> catastrophe. Japan already has one of the world's
> lowest birth rates. Its population of 126 million,
> which has been shrinking for the past decade, is
> projected to plunge a further one-third by 2060.
> Aoyama believes the country is experiencing "a
> flight from human intimacy . . ."[4]

What could be the reason for such a profound flight? There's rarely ever any "catch-all" explanation for a movement, but rather a mixture of little things that, left unattended, all collide at once. While twenty years of economic stagnation followed by a devastating earthquake, tsunami, and nuclear disaster might influence a generation's psyche, Aoyama gave one story of a client she sees on a regular basis that I found particularly interesting: "[She] cites one man in his early 30s, a virgin, who can't get sexually aroused unless he watches female robots on a game similar to *Power Rangers*."

This account seems to sync up well with another article that profiled an anonymous herbivore man in 2020: "In college he became smitten with 'idols'—female starlets who radiate cuteness. What ordinary woman could offer what they did?"[5]

"Idol" is the word Japanese media gives its young female pop stars and models. They are the products of what is known as "hypercuration." Though a strategy called "transmedia" or "media mix," these young women are heavily branded by Japanese entertainment conglomerates, with their likeness appearing everywhere from anime cartoons and games to toys and music. Their lives are tightly controlled by their talent agencies with the goal of presenting a kind of parasocial relationship with consumers.

Idols are personal brands taken to the extreme. They are 1 percent ordinary human and 99 percent shadow. Clearly Japan doesn't own the monopoly on this strategy. US media companies have been hypercurating young pop stars for decades. The more media access points consumers have at their disposal, the easier it becomes. Japan is simply the most advanced and forthright about it.

The idol strategy is built on the intentional blurring of lines between an ordinary person and a fictitious character. The result, when injected at scale into a discontented society, is people who can no longer distinguish between the two and, worse, no longer see the need to.

I once met a successful author who, for whatever reason, seemed bent on trying to "rebrand" himself from the soft-spoken hippy poet he was known as to more of an authoritative business guru. He said to me that in all his previous books, which were memoirs, he was simply presenting a character named after himself, a suit he put on in order to play a part for his audience. I didn't believe it for a second. How tortured one must be, feeling all that pressure to contort one's ordinary identity into some kind of cage for the sake of a manicured public image, a branded shadow. It was like watching a reverse puppet show.

It's easier to navigate the topography of a fictional world we've curated than it is to stumble through the craggy turf of our ordinariness. One only learns to walk tall after learning to walk slow, with an affection for the helping hands in front of and behind him.

Which leads us back to herbivore men. On the surface, their digital, idol-centric lifestyle is easy for them. Their contentment seems evident in the fact that they have no interest in pursuing a partner or raising a family. In actuality, their state of apathy signals a profound *dis*contentment with their actual, physical would-be human mates. When the anonymous young man who confessed his love for idols was asked why he doesn't pursue an ordinary relationship, his reply was, "Why bother? It's a question of risk management."

Let's turn our attention from Japan to another country, Denmark. According to the UN's World Happiness Report, a publication that began in 2012 and draws on global survey data, Denmark consistently scores as one of the happiest cultures on earth.[6] How can such a tiny place, with temperatures below freezing for half the year, be considered one of the most cheerful places to inhabit? The answer lies in the heart of those cold, long, dark winters, not despite them. Many Danes would attribute their reputation to a particular kind of happiness their culture emphasizes, especially during winter months, called *hygge*: a sheltered and secure feeling one gets near old friends, familiar gatherings, and, yes, a warm fireplace.

Hygge comes from a sixteenth-century Norwegian term, *hugga*, which meant "to comfort" or "to console." It's where we derive the English word "hug."[7] The practice of cultivating *hygge* dates as far back as the Middle Ages and was birthed out of a reaction to the blistering harshness of Nordic winters. It's the ritual of becoming close in ordinary sanctuaries, drawing inward and recognizing the common grace in the flicker of a fire and unforgotten friendships. Said in other words, "a roof and walls and fireplace."

In Denmark, even in the twenty-first century, content-ment isn't attempted by trying to simulate an ideal. You won't find Danes viewing images of tropical shores or rocky deserts via virtual headsets or phones as a way to deal with the harshness of winter. Instead, you'll find them with an almost childlike appreciation for what many of us would quickly overlook as ordinary, the generous cover only small things can offer. Rather than detaching from their bodies and the reality surrounding them, they lean further into it all.

By the light of that fire, we can now turn back to the American Dream and see it with clearer eyes. How can we redefine happiness in an age where the temptation is to sim-ply simulate it? The answer hasn't been lacking, only hidden.

To America's founders, the pursuit of "happiness" was squarely unambiguous. It meant striving toward a feeling of self-worth and dignity that one could access freely by con-tributing to their community and civic life. It wasn't about personal status, positioning, or idol worship. It was a beat-itude, concerned mainly with one's ability to invest in the common good of those whose hands are covered with the same soil.

The original American Dream wasn't simply concerned with one's fireplace; it was also concerned with one's neigh-bor's. That's a definition broad and bright enough to spark across multiple centuries and multiverses.

Left solely to our devices and the ones who control them, it's more than possible we'll see an uprising transpire at some point in the twenty-first century. It will either be one of aggression or, worse, a revolution of apathy. To prevent both, the American Dream must take off its jetpack and return to its roots. Once on the ground, we'll remember such a dream can only be effective insofar as it is achievable by its huddled masses. The hope of America is at once a commandment that our fire bear witness to another, and a turning inward to see our shared ordinariness as sanctuary.

05

SENATOR CRUZ AND THE ROBOT MUSE

Media as Public Space

THE FIELDS

Van Gogh painted fields as an act of rebellion
away from the ashen city,
its stone mutations,
factory smog
and pigeon wings.
He chucked a piece of charcoal at the blackened gate
and ran like the Dickens for an opening in the gloom.

Go to the fields in protest.
Spy on a pregnant cattail.
Let it humble you with its influence.
Try to paint whatever seems edgeless
if only to feel your breath collapse
into humility's merciful breast.

Incarnate what you no longer have the strength to ignore.
Dream farther than the edge of your finger.

Beatitude

03.

BLESSED ARE THOSE
WHO URGE MEDIA
TO BEND TOWARD
DEMOCRACY, FOR THEY
SHALL PREVENT THE
OPPOSITE.

On one of the first spring days in 2022, every spare nook and cranny of one of the hearing rooms on Capitol Hill was lined with cameras and screens to cover Supreme Court nominee Ketanji Brown Jackson's judiciary hearing. Jackson sat poised, resolute, her eyes shining with the magnitude of the moment as she answered wide-ranging questions into a long, slender microphone.

Soon the senator from Texas, Ted Cruz, would have his chance to examine the freshly nominated judge. Perched high behind a large wooden desk, he began laying into Judge Jackson, aggressively questioning her on issues he knew would resonate with his constituents. This was to be expected, but now he was going well past his allotted speaking time.

The chair of the Judiciary Committee, Senator Rick Durbin, repeatedly banged his gavel, reminding Cruz that his time had long been finished and pleading with him to wrap up his remarks.

"You can bang it as long as you want," Cruz said as Durbin continually struck his gavel.

"At some point you have to play by the rules," Durbin shot back.

"I know you like to interrupt, but you have consumed a substantial time of my questioning, and I'm going to ask my questions," fired Cruz. "And if you want to testify, you are welcome to."

After the heated exchange, several reporters lunged for their cameras to zoom in on what Cruz did next. One remarked that the senator appeared to be looking down at his phone for an extended period. Another made the bold suggestion that he was checking Twitter. Within seconds, a photojournalist crouching behind the senator managed to secure a smoking gun over-the-shoulder shot. Cruz was indeed searching his own name on Twitter and fishing for mentions.[1]

In a room stacked to the rafters with media technology, one can easily speculate that Cruz's performance was just that: a self-designed spectacle to please an algorithm, achieve validation, and annex one's name brand across the metaverse.

We are living in the age of digital conquest, largely at the expense of our most preciously held institutions.

When a democratic process as substantial and consequential as the induction of a new Supreme Court justice is manipulated and contextualized to fit the rules and formats of media platforms like Twitter, the tail has now wagged the dog so hard you could power a cruise liner with a cocker spaniel.

When we end up serving an algorithm over serving ordinary people, contextualizing and contorting our civics to fit the demands of pocket devices, we've lost the plot to the story that once untangled us from tyranny.

Instead, we now move about a kingdom where we've handed responsibility over to platforms, trusting them to reformat all parts of our life, from our social interactions to our sense of self-worth.

Restaurants now design their lighting around what's best for taking selfies. Graffiti artists no longer make statements, but photo opportunities. Politicians don't ask what's best for people, only what *sounds* best.

The notion that it's the media's world and we're just living in it has become increasingly clear to me the more I've tried to keep up with whatever claims to be "breaking news" at the moment. If Chomsky warned that the media manufactures consent, choosing to spotlight whatever narrative the powerful want us to play into, Big Media's next most imperative aim seems to be manufacturing attention. Why? Because the architecture of these platforms literally requires that a box be filled and a feed be fed. We can no longer afford to be boring or slow, lest we become buried in a feed of nonstop competing ideas. Those who are loudest, crudest, and most jarring will win. The result is, at best, an overemphasis on consistency and intensity at the expense of quality and usefulness.

The format (the confines of our media platforms) is dictating the function (what should and must be said), or, to borrow from Marshall McLuhan, the medium is dictating the message. Under such a hierarchy, useful ideas for the people and by the people drown in messages for the algorithm by the algorithm.

About a year before Ketanji Brown Jackson's nomination hearing, a reformation that has circulated among advocates and activists for some time became more public in the wake of George Floyd's murder and the ensuing protests.

If you take the time to investigate a city's budget, you will often find such a disproportionate allocation of funds toward law enforcement and crime prevention that it begs the question, "Why not redirect some of those funds into preventive programs like better education, small businesses, and community development?" This argument is similar to critiques of the healthcare industry—that it isn't, in fact, in the health and wellness business, but more realistically in the "illness management business." The message of those wishing to reform policing and healthcare—systems designed to protect our communities—is that both are fundamentally reactive versus proactive. But in the case of activists' message following Floyd's murder, instead of that important budgeting message getting clearly communicated, another one got put in its place: "Defund the police."

To be very clear, I am not criticizing that statement for its shock value. And I'm absolutely not saying people shouldn't be angry about the lack of accountability and overreach of power we've repeatedly seen from police in this country. I understand that a response like "defund the police" comes from Black Americans' complete exhaustion at constantly being oppressed coupled with trying to explain themselves over and over and over again to thick-headed people who refuse to change.

What I am suggesting is that this seems to be another classic case of a medium dictating a message. This is a conversation around semiotics. It's about the shape of words and the media we squeeze them into. The truth is, #DefundThe Police fits a whole lot better into a tweet than #Reallocate FundsToPreventiveProgramsInOrderToDecreasePolice ResponsibilityAndIncreaseOverallQualityOfLifeForAll Parties. #DefundThePolice is easier to read, repeat, and react to. It's ready to go viral—which is all well and good for Great Distraction™ platforms whose very business model happens to be commoditizing our data, our privacy, our beliefs, and our reactions.

Until we place our language outside the format of media meant to market mayhem, however, I honestly don't think we are going to be as persuasive as we could be, or ever create the kind of effectual systemic change we desperately want and need. Why? Because some conversations are simply too important and sacred, too multidimensional, to fit the shapes of our most ubiquitous media platforms: boxes with character limits, square images with sharply defined edges, and comment sections designed to push each other down as we lay our own will on top of the last person's voice.

We shouldn't settle for a broken megaphone, a mouthpiece that isn't serving us anymore. Some messages deserve better.

It begs the question, "How exactly did that megaphone get broken in the first place?" When did we arrive at a moment where we all seem so indebted to media technology, where we have to squeeze our passions and petitions into robotic and rigid frameworks? We all seem to recognize there's a beast we've been feeding, but who turned media into a monster in the first place? What was the turning point exactly?

While I believe several cascading events caused this shift, allow me to string together a narrative that begins to answer these questions. I call it "A Tale of Two Ronalds."

Ronald #1: Ronald Coase and the Battle over Broadcast

In the late fifties and sixties, economist Ronald Coase challenged the Federal Communications Commission, better known as the FCC, and their approach to licensing broadcast channels at a relatively inexpensive and insignificant cost to broadcasters. Coase suggested that, just like any other resource (land, oil, steel, etc.), the market should be the one to decide the price of the broadcast spectrum, specifically the segment used for radio transmission (including, it so happens, those that cell networks would use). From an economic standpoint this makes perfect sense, especially since frequencies on that spectrum were limited and scarcity inevitably creates a bidding war. Why shouldn't the government auction them off at the highest value? That's exactly what the FCC eventually did, with broadcasters and communications firms ultimately paying more than $52 billion for these frequencies.[2]

But what about all the positive, educational, and publicly beneficial uses for broadcast that are *non*commercial? While taking Coase's advice to heart may have proven economically favorable, it ultimately solidified media technology's role as primarily a free-market entity without much pushback, a designation I don't believe should ever be automatically assumed. Communication, the transmission of ideas and information from one citizen to another under a democracy, cannot simply be a product. Whether we like it or not, it's a utility.

Ronald #2: Ronald Regan and the Death of the Fairness Doctrine

In 1949, the FCC created the policy known as the Fairness Doctrine to require any broadcast license holder to present controversial public issues in such a way that differing sides were fairly represented. The doctrine had two basic principles:

1. Broadcasters had to devote some portion of their airtime to conversing over controversial matters crucial to public interest.
2. Broadcasters had to air contrasting views when it came to those matters.

Broadcasters were given extensive margin in how much time they should allot and exactly how to provide "contrasting views." Many chose to present these views in the form of news segments, editorial pieces, or public affairs shows.

In the 1980s, however, the Reagan administration began pressuring the FCC, questioning the doctrine's relevance and necessity in an increasingly competitive multimedia landscape. In 1987, the FCC unanimously voted to abolish the Fairness Doctrine, with a reasoning that, in retrospect, might make your head spin. According to the commission, because there were now *numerous* media voices in the marketplace, the Fairness Doctrine seemed unconstitutional, stifling the free speech guaranteed in the First Amendment.[3] No such restriction had been placed on print media, also historically abundant. With the advent of new technology, the agency concluded, the scarcity of airwaves was no longer an issue. Intelligent citizens could access all types of viewpoints from all types of media with incredible ease!

And what could be the problem with that?

Call it shortsighted. Call it caving to political pressure. The irony is uncanny. The reason the FCC gave for ending the Fairness Doctrine is the exact reason why it continues to be necessary.

In 1987, could anyone have predicted the tsunami of info-techno-tainment about to explode as the next decade turned into the next millennium? Perhaps not, but surely some observers were disturbed by what immediately ensued: the rise of two independent cable news channels, FOX

News and MSNBC, burgeoning through America's living rooms and vehicle dashboards with no guidelines to keep them from polarizing an entire generation. These companies, which had the entrepreneurial savvy to seek airwaves that weren't publicly owned or licensed and thus couldn't be regulated, were the early seeds of personality-branded media technology, and became warning signs of the Great Distraction to come. At best, the United States government has been unsuccessful at stabilizing the crisis ever since. At worst, they've fallen entirely asleep at the wheel.

The result is that we're now neck deep in a war we've been ill prepared to resist: the war of hyperbole.

One reason why the FCC commissioners' reasoning was shortsighted was because they failed to understand the difference between our human relationship to print as opposed to other, more passive types of media technology. What makes print different isn't the fact that it's abundant; it's that it's *contemplative*.

When we consume print, it activates our hippocampus, the part of the brain responsible for formulating long-term memories. Reading print is a solitary, imaginative process, one that requires disciplined and active participation. When we consume media via a screen with multiple entry and exit points vying for our attention, we're using more of our brain's temporal lobe, which manages short-term memory. The more attention we give to media that engages the temporal lobe, the less we work our contemplative, critical muscle.[4] Yes, the increasing accessibility of media creates remarkable opportunities—but they carry a price: the more media, the more overwhelm, the less critical thinking. The increase in media variety demands more prudence and nuance, not less.

Even though our twenty-first-century media landscape now looks vastly different, we shouldn't discard the FCC's approach to America's growing obsession with media technology before Ronald Coase and Ronald Reagan elbowed their way inside. The creation of the Fairness Doctrine seemed to establish this underlying creed that media technology, when it exists outside the confines of paper and print, is both a fragile and potent thing and therefore ought to be judiciously bounded, so as not to bring about a Great Distraction. The logic was that broadcast media should exist in a democracy to serve the will of ordinary citizens rather than those citizens existing to serve it.

I believe there is still time to bring that sense of reverence into the nuanced and complex landscape we find ourselves in, beginning with three choices.

First, we can put our energy toward creating private space rather than defaulting to megaphones.

Every wedding ceremony I've had the pleasure of attending has had one thing in common with the rest. No, I'm not talking about rings or vows or kisses or expensive clothes people only wear once. I'm talking about feedback. And not the kind some estranged aunt gives when commenting on how cheap the flowers look. I mean the kind that comes from audio-related technical difficulties, mainly abrupt, loud squeals during an otherwise intimate moment. If not feedback, then at least a minister who realizes only after a few crucial sentences into their welcome speech that they forgot to turn their microphone's battery pack on, or an acoustic guitar that keeps cutting out for some bizarre reason even the hired sound engineer can't seem to figure out. It seems universal.

Knowing this, I had one request for the ceremony where I would marry my soon-to-be-wife, Kelly: that there be no amplification. Zero. My thought was that these vows were between Kelly, me, and God. If those who attended got to listen in, too, great! It would already be a stressful day leading up to it. Why leave room for what I'd found, in my experience, to be an inevitable distraction? Besides, I assumed it would probably be a small wedding anyway.

A few hundred RSVPs later, I wondered if I had made a huge mistake.

Our ceremony was in a sprawling park outside San Diego where Kelly had grown up going to church picnics. Rows of folding chairs were arranged in the round. In the center stood my bride, myself, our closest friends, the minister, and some musicians.

Perhaps to some people's surprise, as the sun shone down on our little ritual, you could hear a pin drop between the minister's words. It was even quieter when our friend sang one of our favorite songs. The level of silence when we exchanged the vows we'd written each other was holy. Even the birds held their beaks.

It was quiet because *we* were quiet. Everyone was literally on the edge of their seats leaning in to listen to the sound of small stones casting widening ripples into a great stillness.

Unamplified conversations require people lean in to listen. Media is often most influential on the micro level, focused on the few versus the many, when the goal is specificity rather than scalability. It's become a completely foreign concept to suggest that just because you've manifested an idea in your head, you don't need to share that idea online, openly, for everyone to see in perpetuity. The allure to perform, to manufacture influence, to please the Robot Muse has usurped the far more influential drive to learn, understand, contemplate, and imagine.

These smaller kinds of conversations, which don't fit neatly into boxes, and are held more often under fluorescent lights rather than camera lights, local establishments rather than global platforms, in front of faces rather than screens, are generally more productive. They inhabit a format strong enough to include and consider a multitude of diverse voices rather than simply the loudest or most bombastic. Communication without the allure of amplifying one's personal brand, focused on changing a mind rather than creating a spectacle, is a more democratic method of communication than our corporate algorithms provide. That insight may seem simple, but until we favor unamplified discussions over the alternative by making better civic choices it will remain just an insight. These kinds of choices (open primaries and term limits easily come to mind) might just result in the kinds of leaders who could restore the Fairness Doctrine, call the loudest media platforms to a higher standard with legislation, and foster space for unamplified discussions to flourish.

Yes, a message can travel far across connected devices, but it will often resonate deeper when shared directly among connected people. Every time we are tempted to share a passionate thought with the entire world, we could redirect that impulse toward a private conversation. Call it a moment of contemplative action. Call it a quiet rebellion. We can choose to kindly send a private message to someone we disagree with instead of perpetuating our culture's default method of shaming them publicly. As we'll discuss in a later chapter, we can start the conversation not by attempting degradation, but reconciliation. No matter how justified we may feel in calling someone out in front of everyone, we can flip the knee-jerk outrage on its head and recognize it for the broken megaphone it is. We can educate our kids to prioritize private communication when using media, especially when in conflict. We can let them know some conversations are too important to be controlled by algorithms. We can believe the ripples that form whenever a few convene with genuine curiosity and good faith create their own virality beneath the surface.

This happened in the seventeenth century. It can be argued that the "Republic of Letters" was one of the first iterations of a media-driven social network, perhaps even an early version of the metaverse. Described as "a metaphysical thing in that it was an idea more than it was a place," the Republic of Letters was the name a group of intellectuals across Europe and America gave to their letter-writing club. The collective would exchange essays with each other about various topics of cultural importance ranging from philosophy and politics to art and economics. Those who considered themselves contributors to the Republic included English philosopher John Locke, Italian humanist Francesco Barbaro, and French linguist Pierre Bayle, as well as several scientists, philosophers, lawyers, and courtiers.

A decentralized, high-diameter network, the Republic of Letters was essentially an open-source platform, welcome to anyone who was able to exercise what the founders held as the two main attributes of citizenship: writing and reading.[5] This global exchange of ideas was slow, thoughtful, and exacting. Those who participated pored over every letter, giving each one careful time, attention, thought, and detail before sending it off to the next member. Some members even had ornate writing desks built specifically for this kind of contemplative practice.

What strikes me most about the Republic of Letters is just how effective it was at advancing Enlightenment ideas globally. And yet the entire network was extremely decentralized. In fact, when data scientists at Stanford began mapping the global correspondence of these letters, they were dumbfounded by certain correlations. One researcher, Dan Edelstein, pointed out, "Anyone who's studied Voltaire and the Enlightenment knows that the French had this almost mythical idea of England as the land of religious freedom, toleration, and this great political system. And yet when you look at the letters, Voltaire is hardly corresponding with anyone in the country and the people he *is* corresponding with are really not who you would expect."[6]

In an era of detailed dashboards and instant analytics, a moment when we can say something we think others will validate and then immediately check to confirm whether they have (even if it's regarding who the next Supreme Court justice should be), it may be vulnerable to admit that growth is not always immediately measurable. Sometimes, as with Voltaire's influence, you map it and it doesn't quite make sense. In hindsight, sustainable, abiding growth is a more quiet, specific, and intimate thing than what an algorithm might show.

The second choice we can make is to start developing public space in the metaverse.

Several years after Ronald Coase composed the justification the FCC ultimately used to privatize airwaves, President Lyndon B. Johnson signed the Public Broadcasting Act of 1967 to help curb that assumption I mentioned earlier: that a force as vast and powerful as media was squarely in the control of the free market. Here's what he had to say upon signing the bill:

> It announces to the world that our nation wants more than just material wealth; our nation wants more than a "chicken in every pot." We in America have an appetite for excellence, too. While we

work every day to produce new goods and to create new wealth, we want most of all to enrich man's spirit. That is the purpose of this act. It will give a wider and, I think, stronger voice to educational radio and television by providing new funds for broadcast facilities. It will launch a major study of television's use in the Nation's classrooms and its potential use throughout the world.[7]

What came next was the golden age *of Sesame Street, Mister Rogers' Neighborhood, Reading Rainbow, News-Hour, NOVA, Great Performances*, and so on. These were brilliant programs designed for twentieth-century living rooms. But here in the twenty-*first* century, it's been difficult to identify how these good intentions, which once flourished through the medium of radio and television, translate to our current pocket-sized and hyperconnected digital landscape. There seems to have been a lack of policy innovation and forethought, let alone any sense of collaboration between policy makers and the technology and communication giants in the open market (unless you count Google and Apple providing cheap or free computers to young, impressionable school kids—in which case, what could possibly be wrong with that?).

As we continue to build the scaffolding of the metaverse, already buzzing with corporate kingdoms and personal brands, we also ought to advocate for a generous allocation of public space therein. Imagine what that might look like!

In the way libraries were once esteemed as brick-and-mortar beacons of human intellect and contemplation, perhaps public space in the metaverse would look like commissioning media makers to design experiences that draw us back to the best humankind has to offer itself. In the way parks promote peace and tranquility, free from the congestion and pollution of highways and industrialization, such public online space might be free from algorithms that reward the loudest voices, designed instead to foster dialogue between differing ones. Such mediums could be designed with curiosity as their highest value, with the intent to understand, empathize, and seek common ground. People can use the best of our media tools to connect, learn, document, and share, creating digital bridges and planting "meta-farms."

To take this a step further, we now live in an era marked by the "clipification" of all things—fragments of quotes and micro-events ripped from their context, living instead as individual bites for all to snap up at no meaningful end.

At its best, the trend of video getting shorter, smaller, faster, and punchier has yielded a generation with no patience for any event that requires more than a moment to contemplate without stimulation. At its worst, this shift toward hyperterse video has spawned a global pandemic of misinformation and unquenchable outrage among people who no longer have the patience or tools to investigate its missing context. It simply elicits a quick, addictive, emotional reaction. In short, what gets clipified gets commercialized.

We've been so focused for so long on whittling our messages down to their pithiest and punchiest elements in the hopes of their thriving in the marketplace of attention that we've forgotten how important it is to contemplate them. Why not design and designate public platforms that require any videos uploaded to be at least three minutes long? Why not create a "context box"—a spot that requires users to write at least three hundred characters explaining the video's context? Algorithms could boost longer videos or those whose context boxes appear the most accurate. For starters, these guidelines would make us better thinkers. They also would force our attention spans to expand, training us to sit with an idea for longer than a few seconds and give it the breathing room it deserves before we form our opinions. Last, even though each clip would be longer, it potentially would keep us off our devices more, by tempering our addiction to endlessly scroll to the next clip-mercial and race against each other to annex the metaverse with our instant thoughts.

This is ultimately why some amount of public space, if not greater overall regulation of the private sector, is important. If we're being honest, any reform that results in people devoting *less* time to their devices simply isn't in the best interest of Great Distraction™ corporations. Capitalism without criteria is just another clip without context.

Some theorists call for a completely decentralized internet, created strictly by the people and for the people—end of story. While I understand the intention and agree that a web that bends toward decentralization is far better than one with overcentralized power, either in corporate or government hands, a purely libertarian approach has a few issues of its own. For starters, the genie is already well out of the bottle when it comes to the current state of digital centralization, from the devices we use to the platforms they display. Completely undoing that all might be ideal, even the goal, but is probably impossible (in the same way a pure meritocracy might be ideal if it weren't for a history of men deliberately making decisions that kept generations of other men from enjoying the same level ground they do). Precedents have been set, damage done, communities commoditized. Therefore, at least some amount of government collaboration is necessary. The intentional designation of some public discourse space would be a worthy service to a generation who grew up knowing only a polluted metaverse. Even if the internet were to wind up truly and permanently decentralized, it would take the will of the people voting for a government that mandated it be so. The metaverse doesn't have to be completely decentralized for it to be democratic. I'm not sure I know one libertarian who's seen Yellowstone and wishes it could become a subdivision of condominiums lined with Astroturf.

Last, we can choose to make news boring again. Or at least more boring than it is right now. We've seen the consequences of revoking the Fairness Doctrine: the rise of loud, exciting, super-branded, hypercurated personalities positioning themselves as authorities on current events. They may not be teenagers who sing pop music and guest star in anime (although I would definitely watch a current-events show with that premise), but they are idols in their own right, garnering massive fanbases and convincing them that their ideology is their identity. The forgotten art of being ordinary hinges on the difficult work of untangling the two. An identity that can stand apart from an ideology is kryptonite to idol culture.

Layer the rise of the internet's most ubiquitous social media platforms (whose algorithms incentivize drama) with the rise of "outrage personalities," and you have the climate we're all familiar with and weary of, where "infotainment" now stands in for facts and standards. Call it Death by Hot Take.

As journalist Kat Tenbarge put it in her analysis of the widely broadcasted (and hypercurated) defamation trial between two famous actors,

> A pitfall of going to YouTubers and TikTokers for coverage is that these creators aren't beholden to any editorial standards or journalistic norms. In fact, they're incentivized to break them, to fit the narrative and make money . . . Unfortunately, social media incentivizes us to care very, very much about what other people think of us. This has a net negative effect on social progress, because progress is rarely popular in the moment.[8]

Similarly, in a 2021 slander lawsuit against a popular cable news personality, the judge made the following statement, heavily basing the ruling on the arguments of the cable network's own lawyers:

> The "general tenor" of the show should
> then inform a viewer that [the personality]
> is not "stating actual facts" about the topics
> he discusses and is instead engaging in
> "exaggeration" and "non-literal commentary."[9]

That argument may have won in court, but when it comes to the court of public opinion, these personalities clearly have outsized and outmatched influence. We grieve democracy when the most influential voices are simply the most "exaggerated." We shouldn't leave it up to the "general tenor" of a show to inform the viewer that something masking itself as news is, in reality, not.

When everything can be considered journalism, nothing is. Instead, we should require distribution platforms from social media to cable news to create clear and up-front categories and labels for their personalities who swim in the sea of current events, especially once their followers reach a certain threshold of potential viral impact. We'll talk more about how better categories and labels can help us navigate the metaverse in the next chapter, but for now, this might look like a short disclaimer at the top of a show or more specific subcategories for a podcast. For example, the widely heard and wildly controversial podcaster Joe Rogan falls under the category of "Society" on the platform of his distributor, Spotify. That feels too broad for how influential his commentary has become. Perhaps "Entertainment" or "Opinion" would be a more fitting category for a comedian and MMA fighter.

Would these tweaks change much? Perhaps not. We can't say for certain until we try. But they feel like practical and attainable ways to prioritize public interest without decimating profits or flirting with censorship. Media companies could protect free speech while also providing helpful context. These labels wouldn't need to carry as negative a tone as, say, the surgeon general's tobacco warning. We don't have to say "These opinions will kill you," even though, when taken as gospel, they just might (see the anti-vax movement during the COVID pandemic).

Of course, this would cause media networks of all kinds to create clearer standards for what qualifies as journalism and news. In that case, the original standards provided by the Fairness Doctrine should be reimagined and reinstated as the minimum threshold for journalistic integrity and excellence.

We're all starting to feel the fragility of squeezing everything our ancestors bled for on battlefields and union lines, in marches and underneath cold rock, into a format designed to entertain and distract us . . . the fatigue it brings and the confusion it breeds without pause. Ordinary life may not be as polished or punchy, but the trade-off is a depth and breadth uncontainable by a camera frame; the bewildering complexity, unlikely friendships, and crooked mysteries too angular and multidimensional to cram within the edges of a screen. We the people are too robust to be manipulated. Democracy is too fragile a thing to dramatize. There's a sea change upon us. But to see that change through, we need to become better at identifying a certain distinction: not strictly between what's real and what's squarely make-believe, but a more nuanced separation. We must become better at identifying the difference between "real" and things pretending to be real *without our knowledge*—something professional wrestlers call "kayfabe."

06

WRESTLING KILLED THE REALITY STAR

Media as Kayfabe

YOUR STRENGTH

You know it deep inside you.
May you doubt a thousand things but never that.
Let it steady and guide you home instantly.
Do not search for my voice
(or perhaps the voice you might wish I had)
when lies disguise themselves
and try to disguise you as well.
But look for yours alone,
not far off on some unreachable island
or locked behind some brink.
There is a strength that begins
in the dust you were made from
and branches out
broader than your body
for you to run freely in
or sit
or lie down—
whatever you know it's meant for.

Beatitude

04.

BLESSED ARE
THOSE WHO HELP
DISTINGUISH TRUTH
FROM FICTION, FOR
THEY SHALL BE
CALLED ARTISTS.

I met David a few years back in a sleepy little town outside Boulder, Colorado. A local dance company had read my previous book and decided to create a show around it (a sentence I never thought I'd write, especially considering I don't think of my writing as being the kind one dances to). The company asked David to compose its music, and he accepted. We got to talking backstage and quickly realized we had a lot in common. We were both fans of mystic contemplatives like Thomas Merton and John O'Donohue, loved the poetry of Rilke and Wendell Berry, and had an unhealthy obsession with vinyl records. If I'm honest, his knowledge of all these subjects surpassed mine by a long shot, which probably made me come off like an annoying, slightly intimidated little brother. If I did, he didn't seem to care. My wife and

I found ourselves spending most of the following day with David, winding through the bakeries and antique stores of their main street and listening to records in his home studio.

What I appreciate most about David is how he carries himself. He's tall, bulky, with flecks of gray seasoning his long wispy hair and dusting his five o'clock shadow. His light eyes never stray far from you when he's speaking with you, and his voice . . . well, his voice is what fascinates me the most. I don't think I've ever heard David speak louder than slightly above a whisper. To have a conversation with David is to enter into a brick room with a roaring fireplace in the middle of a Denmark winter. In some people this would translate as shyness, intimidation, or self-consciousness, as if they had never found the echo of their unfettered voice to begin with. But with David, his low-decibel countenance comes across as confident and interested, capable of booming and yelling but bored with that particular expression. It doesn't seem forced, but I imagine it's learned.

Perhaps all the shouting took him as far as it was capable of taking him at some point in his youth. Perhaps, standing on that threshold, he realized it wasn't all he imagined it could be. Perhaps he realized turning his own volume down created a certain generosity that suited both his own ears and those around him.

David, after all, is an exceptional music producer and composer. Married to his quiet, listening spirit is an unwavering curiosity about how it all works, and by "all" I mean *all*—music, electricity, biology, the cosmos.

The other day, for example, while we were catching up, he started to go off on a tangent about some new instrument cables he recently purchased for his studio. That's when he said something I had never heard before. He explained that when it came to cabling, it doesn't really matter very much what kind of metal is used for the wiring. Sure, silver is better than copper and they're both a little frailer than gold, but they all basically perform the same function of conducting electricity. When it comes to sound, what makes for a quality cable is its capacity to silence noise. A well-crafted, insulated cable will block out all the frequencies and murmurs in the air to allow the purest sound to shine through. In other words, it helps an instrument sound most like itself.

The advent of the twenty-first century may have turned us into a culture of live wires, but even as we grow tired of the noise, the static, the competing frequencies, we have the chance to repair and reimagine our connections. Then we can do the difficult but liberating work of transmitting our truest, most human, most ordinary identities between each other, choosing them over our supersized shadows.

Before we can do this, we must continue to disentangle the two. This, I believe, is at the heart of our postmodern conundrum. Truth eludes us because we elude our ordinary selves. When we inhabit multiple realities, incarnate multiple narratives simultaneously without some kind of reserved reverence or regard for our foundational one, we end up choosing whatever version seems to benefit us the most. Is it any wonder why we find ourselves on a different plane than our neighbor?

Better language can help us.

Words have always been the greatest asset of the ordinary. Words are cheap and outperform their cost when spent wisely. They've instigated revolutions, mobilized masses, and perhaps most importantly, won the impenetrable heart. As we journey further into the twenty-first-century metaverse, our shared task is to help each other identify just what we mean when we communicate. For example, terms like "augmented reality" and "virtual reality" by their nomenclature seem to assume that reality itself can be augmented and virtualized. This is a deep and crucial misunderstanding, void of the kind of anchor we seek. Instead, replacing the word "reality" with "environment" would be clearer. I get this kind of language fussing may sound like splitting hairs, but I'd argue it might accomplish something far more substantial: recalibrate our True North. If we fail to give each other the gift of better bearings with clearer markings, especially our children who will inherit the worlds and narratives we've created, we will continue to miss each other—losing the sacred commonality of our natural humanity, and confusing each other instead for mere shadows made of pixels and glass. In other words, we will be unable to identify the real from the make-believe.

Part of helping become each other's clearest, most vibrant signals is increasing our understanding of the difference between the illusion and the real thing—what's pretend and what isn't. As it stands right now, there's too much noise to separate the two. We're like Alice, constantly passing through the looking glass into another paradigm. The difference is we've made so many journeys back and forth, we're not sure which side is real and which is imaginary.

Why is the noise so deafening? How did our cultural vernacular get so subjective and meaningless? Let's briefly sketch out the history of the complicated relationship between media and make-believe.

This inclination to blur the line between pretend and reality has long been a drug of choice for any media maker regardless of what century they call home. That rush, that feeling of validation and success that comes with fooling your audience, is so powerful that you're tempted to never let them in on the secret, especially if you believe doing so may hurt your chances of fooling a new audience the next town over.

A long-standing example of this kind of secret keeping can be found in the history of professional wrestling. Since its beginnings as a traveling sideshow in the early 1900s, professional wrestling has held on to a sacred insider term, a private code name designated only for those in their industry: kayfabe. Kayfabe (perhaps "be fake" in pig Latin) was a "wink-and-nod" term among insiders signaling that their competitions, though presented to audiences as legitimate, were in fact scripted and staged. Not only did this apply to matches but to the wrestlers themselves, a distinction into which the industry began to lean even harder during the 1980s and '90s, when professional wrestling found a new, booming audience: children. During this golden age for the sport, celebrity wrestlers were instructed by their higher-ups to stay in character in public at all times—during media appearances, in the ring, and even while interacting with young fans. Wrestlers were also expected to maintain fictitious rivalries with their opponents, strategically architected feuds that were branded as legitimate for impressionable audiences, even outside the ring.[1]

Kayfabe was the strategy and it worked.

This concept of kayfabe, I'm convinced, is what Plato was so irritated about in *The Republic* when he depicts Socrates going after "the poet" with unceasing vitriol. Before you balk at any sentence that would conflate pro wrestler and poet, Plato's poet isn't the kind our modern sensibilities would describe, the one who prods, provokes, rhymes, and reveals. Instead, I think what Plato seemed particularly frustrated by were ancient forms of kayfabe. In his 1963 book, *Preface to Plato,* the classicist Eric A. Havelock expounds (brackets are my own commentary):

> For this training [of the intellect] depends on the skill of calculation and measurement; the illusions of sensible experience are critically corrected by the controlling reason. Poetry [insert "kayfabe"] *per contra* indulges in constant illusionism, confusion, and irrationality. This is what *mimesis* ultimately is, a shadow-show of

phantoms like those images seen in the darkness on the wall of the cave.

For Plato, reality is rational, scientific, and logical, or it is nothing. The poetic medium [conjure images of Hulk Hogan and the Kardashians rather than Langston Hughes or Emily Dickinson], so far from disclosing the true relations of things or the true definitions of the moral virtues, forms a kind of refracting screen which disguises and distorts reality and at the same time distracts us and plays tricks with us by appealing to the shallowest of our sensibilities.

Speaking of refracting screens and shallow sensibilities, not long after professional wrestling's late-twentieth-century media boom with young viewers, the reality-television format became a mainstream hit, in eerie rhythm with the turn of the twenty-first century. This was kayfabe in primetime.

I'm not sure the history of reality television is necessarily a linear one. One can certainly include televised professional wrestling in its evolution or trace its roots back as early as the 1940s with the success of *Candid Camera* and the Miss America pageant (an earlier form of hypercuration and idol making). One might also be remiss in excluding the selective and hypercurated televising of the Vietnam War, the first war to be broadcast and beamed into people's living rooms in semi–real time. And one might further point to the early 1970s documentary series *An American Family*, which captured a real-life middle-class family living in a Californian suburb, and which was curated down from three hundred hours of footage to just twelve episodes in ways that sparked debate from within the family and among those in the media over the ethics of this unprecedented kind of programming.[2]

We know without a doubt, however, that the genre known to the general public as "reality television" took off in the late 1990s and early 2000s with the introduction of MTV's *Real World* and its primetime broadcast-network successor *Big Brother*. Both featured several strangers living under the same roof as their main premise. They positioned ordinary people as "characters" without explicitly letting viewers in on this strategy. Kayfabe. That novel late-twentieth-century decision is the single most important artifact in helping us understand everything that feels off with media in the twenty-first.

I'm not wanting to sound like the language police, but here we are again at a crisis of words and definitions. The calculated labeling (branding, if you will) of individuals as characters we're made to fall in love with, *without* calling them characters, is the instigating media strategy that has produced multiple generations' worth of confusion and conflict. It's the transition from Walter Cronkite to Tucker Carlson, or the other way around, from *The Addams Family* to the Kardashians. Paradoxically, as nonfiction storytelling became more fictitious, fictional storytelling started becoming hyperrealistic. This is Marshall McLuhan's "Reverse" law in action, part of his "Four Laws of Media Tetrad," the theory he developed in the fifties and sixties that led him to predict that an actor would become president within the next fifteen years (enter Ronald Reagan stage right, followed by the twenty-first-century version, Donald Trump, a reality star). The "Reverse" law is what happens when a medium eventually becomes so saturated it ends up having the opposite effect of its original intent.

If audiences were escaping through infotainment and reality television, producers realized, then fiction needed to do more than amuse the senses—it had to jar them. Consider the progression from the exaggerated portrayal of crime on *Magnum, P.I.* to the hyperrealistic *Breaking Bad*. Better yet, look at Adam West's campy comfort version of Batman in the 1960s versus Christopher Nolan's gritty twenty-first-century adaptation. Even Tim Burton's take in the late eighties now seems almost excessively whimsical.

In near lockstep progression, soon after reality TV as we now know it started to take off, so did the internet—a place that, on the one hand, broke down the proverbial "fourth wall" between media gatekeepers and audiences by generating a wave of authenticity and truth telling, while also allowing for the commoditization of line-blurring at warp speed. Call it "Do-It-Yourself-Kayfabe."

Shortly after my daughter started kindergarten, she would come home talking nonstop about someone named JoJo Siwa.

JoJo (Joelle Joanie Siwa) is a real person. However, she's been "super-positioned" by corporate brands looking to sell products to parents. My daughter's friends had JoJo backpacks, JoJo shoes, JoJo sweatshirts, and JoJo dolls. The result is that JoJo, not unlike a pro wrestler or a Japanese idol, plays a character in the media she creates—except there's an extra layer of confusion: She's not telling my daughter that.

Even as a kid, I sort of knew names like Jake the Snake and Sting couldn't be the names their parents gave to them. I was pretty sure Jake didn't emerge from the womb of some poor woman holding a giant python. And I had a feeling Sting wasn't born with black-and-white stripes from his cheeks up to his forehead.

JoJo, however, seems to embody a new level of kay-fabe. To my daughter, JoJo is just being Joelle Joanie, your average teenage girl who posts videos about her life and becomes wildly famous.

JoJo was named one of *Time* magazine's most influential people in 2020. Her online videos and subscribers have amassed hundreds of millions of views. JoJo started off as a dancer. In some of her videos she sings. However, her main "schtick" is simply talking (yelling, really), being a loud, excited teenage girl. Her influence is being an influencer. Her brand is being a brand. And what exactly platformed all this viral success in the first place? In 2013, she was a contestant on *Dance Moms*, a reality show.

When my daughter first started mentioning JoJo, wanting to watch her videos and own her accessories, I began browsing some of her videos. Several uploads had positive messages, like her music video in which she rejected bullying. Others gave me pause. One in particular featured her giving viewers a tour around her house. Inside, the normal suburban single-family home was decorated to the nines with framed posters of the star and shelves littered with her own line of merchandise, available exclusively at Target. In her living room, a gumball machine stood next to a giant arcade crane game filled with more toys and accessories. Noticeably lacking were any family photos or furniture to sit on, almost as if no parents or siblings occupied the structure for its intended residential function—you know, a home.

Another video spotlights JoJo showing off a brand new BMW 4 Series car wrapped with her name and likeness. This, I should point out, was all shortly before *newer* posts showcasing her family's recent move to a $3.45 million California mansion. These videos also feature cross-branded references to her partnership with a television network and merchandise line.

When you're engaging JoJo Siwa through media, you are not engaging a person, you're engaging a strategy, one where the lines between real life and promotion are no longer detectable. JoJo is not an ordinary teenager. She's kayfabe.

It's difficult enough for adults to distinguish between what's real and fake on the internet. A kindergartener absolutely doesn't know any better. They don't have the neuro-capacity to understand hyper-positioning or kayfabe; they just see a teenage girl named JoJo who started posting her videos online (something they could do as well) and simply wants to show them around her house, a shrine to her success. By the way, in many ways this house seems to resemble the perfect dream house, not for the typical sixteen-year-old, but oddly, for a demographic several years younger.

Children are naturally inclined to mirror what they admire. In JoJo's case, they may attempt to publish their own online media, without ever understanding the complex hierarchical infrastructure behind creating a strategic brand like "JoJo Siwa"—and fail as a result. One could naturally draw a direct line from that kind of disappointment and disillusion to the unprecedented levels of anxiety and depression kids are now facing. No longer do they look up to blatantly fictional symbols like Batman or Barbie (both fraught with problems in their own right, steeped as they are in twentieth-century thinking). Rather, twenty-first-century kids are looking to figures whom they perceive as ordinary people, who are simply documenting their lives, exercising their creativity, and reaping the rewards.

I can hear you. All this language policing and criticism of what "kids these days" are watching is starting to sound a little "get-off-my-lawnish." I get it. But stick with me. Because that's not my intent at all.

I don't reference these examples to enshrine the good old days, hoping that we somehow revert to them. Rather, I'm trying to broadcast from a future moment—perhaps eighty years into the twenty-first century, standing over a lookout and seeking to identify where we started preferring fiction over facts, translucent holograms we could see but couldn't touch, as if that forgotten sense wasn't connected to our deepest, most primal longings. I'm attempting to draw us a road map for the future: how we pivoted, how we changed, how we greeted the rest of the century with a greater understanding of our relationship with the metaverse, a wiser sense, of our own autonomy.

This is the reason why I'm such a big advocate for clearer language—categories, identifiers, and labels. This blurring between fiction and reality is at the heart of our fractured relationship with media technology. This isn't news to most of us. Just as you know cigarettes hold no nutritional value or that the earth's climate seems to be getting drastically more volatile every year, you are most likely aware of the dangers of kayfabe even if you couldn't label it until now. But because you now have better language for it, you can call out its influence more easily in your life and the lives of those you care about. Better identifiers can lead to healthier identities.

With that, there's one more language observation before we start crafting the road map forward. It has to do with what we think about when we think of the word *game*.

Many media technology platforms, owned by public corporations that rose to ubiquity in the early 2000s, still position themselves to users as communities. This may be how they started out, but to continue calling them that sends us back into another crisis of definitions. Instead, they have very much become games. Within their ecosystems, there are winners and losers, depending on what we, the users, do or don't do, what kind of media we create, and how quickly we're able to adapt to the changing rules. The more we inhabit these platforms—commenting, interacting, and posting—the more their various algorithms reward us. While the leaders of these platforms may argue that this is intended to preserve a sense of community rather than perpetuating a self-seeking "look at me" fest, it also conveniently incentivizes us to remain inside the app and stay active there as often as we possibly can.

To be clear, it's perfectly fine for a platform to be a game, if that's what it truly is. Games are not only fun; playing them is hardwired into our human psyches. We begin wading into the murky waters of kayfabe, however, when the rules aren't completely transparent or can change at any point a platform decides they should. In 2021, the CEO of Instagram, Adam Mosseri, wrote a public post to explain from thirty thousand feet how the application's algorithms work while promising to be more transparent in the future. The post reads more like a public relations effort to get ahead of negative press, but it does make a key admission: that the company indeed prioritizes and ranks posts based on popularity. There is an inherent competition residing in the code of Instagram, but to the average user, especially a child whose brain is still developing, it's not a game. It's positioned as a "social network," a meta–meeting space to connect with friends who might eventually become fans.

A recent report found that girls who increased their time on social media were more apt than boys to admit they were dissatisfied with their lives at a slightly earlier age.[3] In a similar study, boys actually reported higher overall screen usage than girls, but the way each gender used those screens differed. Boys mainly played video games, while girls spent more time using social networks and texting.[4]

Perhaps the reason boys are slightly less prone to depression and anxiety due to media technology is because they spend slightly more time experiencing metaverse worlds like Fortnite, which they know are fictional. Once we perceive something as a game to win, we can work toward defeating it. We can use social media platforms to win against tyrannical governments or a virtual headset to master performing a life-saving heart surgery. Games that lead to cherishing the miraculously ordinary human being are games worth sweating over. Games that confuse people for pieces and pawns are not.

There was a wild story a few years ago about two seventeen-year-old boys playing Fortnite together. One lived in the UK and the other in Texas. While they were playing, the boy in Texas began suffering a seizure. The UK boy immediately looked up how to alert medical authorities in the US and consequently saved his friend's life.

Now, contrast that with a story my friend told me the other day. His teenage son had been giving out his family's physical address to opponents he met on Fortnite. Apparently, the competition had gotten so heated that the boy said something to the tune of "Why don't you come over to my house and say that to my face?" Thankfully, no one decided to take him up on the offer.

In one case, the breaking of boundaries between people who live thousands of miles away from each other carried with it the power to save a life. In another case, the inability to create a healthy understanding between "game" and "reality" could have proven dangerous.

Another fellow dad recently shared with me *his* Fortnite story in which his teenage son felt so attached to his avatar, his character shadow, that when a friend made fun of its name, he felt as if the friend were making fun of him. After all, even though he knew it was a fictional character, it was still his voice moving its mouth, his controls swinging its arms, his intuition telling him where to go and what not to do. It was part extension and part fantasy. And it was confusing.

In the metaverse, ordinary people both young and old would be better off playing the kinds of games where they either inhabit characters that are extraordinarily different from themselves or ones where they are incentivized to embody their genuine, imperfectly human incarnations. Even if neither is 100 percent unattainable, why not make them our design guidelines?

In the meantime, if designers are going to continue creating media that on the one hand is fictional (whether explicitly so or not) and on the other hand encourages people to socialize within that fictional setting, we need to become better at helping the next generation navigate that nuanced terrain. Many media technology giants, however, instead of protecting players, have been treating them as guinea pigs. In fact, some of the fastest-growing companies are gaming platforms like Epic (the creators of Fortnite) and Roblox, which have two things in common: (1) they are building the bones of what the metaverse will look like, and (2) their primary users are children.[5] According to a CNBC report,

> Online gaming companies [like] Roblox and Epic Games . . . have already built virtual worlds, where millions socialize, play and take part in a digital economy. All that to say: the metaverse is already here in a lot of ways. It just hasn't matured and spread beyond a core group of kids and teens, who play Fortnite, Roblox and Minecraft with the same vigor that many of their elders scroll Twitter and binge Netflix.[6]

If kindergarten for my daughter was all about JoJo Siwa, first grade was all about Roblox. She begged my wife and me to create an account for her and install the gaming platform on the family iPad. Can you blame her? Roblox touts about 32 million users, half of them kids under thirteen. Half. Here's another way to measure Roblox's influence: 75 percent of kids in America between the ages of nine and twelve are on it.

So again, I put on my curious-dad hat and began researching. For those as unaware as I was, let me give you a little under-the-hood primer on this wildly successful app. Roblox is essentially a meta-marketplace for game creators and consumers. Game creators can design and sell games to users (most of whom are kids). These games are mostly role-playing games, or, more accurately for the metaverse era, world-building games. An entire economy exists within those worlds where users are encouraged to interact with one another, buying, selling, and trading digital items that help the user either (a) build the world in that game, or (b) build or alter the identity of their avatar through digital items like hair, hats, or sunglasses. Users can spend real money (sometimes unexpectedly racking up their parents' credit card bill) or credits they earn through winning game levels (raising interesting questions about merit, shortcuts, and equity), or they can trade items with other users (which has resulted in multiple user-generated scams and manipulative practices).

As mentioned, Roblox is essentially the metaverse 1.0, a testing ground for the future of immersive media technology with its user-generated world-building economy. The obvious problem is that they're experimenting on children.

Roblox comes with an always-growing suite of parental controls, including the ability for parents to turn off its interactive features. A quick toggle prevents your kids from talking to other users and vice versa. There's just one challenge with that: the entire infrastructure of Roblox is based on user interaction and discovery. My kid wanted to play Roblox because she wanted to play it *with her friends*. Turning off its interactive feature instantly makes Roblox a whole lot less fun. There's also another big problem—you may have already guessed it. At least at the time of this writing, Roblox requires verification for adult users. However, there is no way to verify users under age thirteen. Most of Roblox's parental settings are only enacted once a parent decides to turn them on or off. This means anyone can set up a Roblox account and pose as a child with full access to most of its interactive features.

"One of the things I absolutely know, because I talk to parents and I talk to our community, day in and day out, is that parents and teachers don't even know that account restrictions exist," said Roblox's vice president of civility and partnerships, Tami Bhaumik, in an interview with *Venture Beat*. "If there's not a basic education level, then there's always going to be a problem."[7]

I don't believe the creators of these metaverse games are inherently insidious. They're just the latest in a long line of media makers who have become comfortable with the concept of kayfabe as strategy. And kayfabe isn't concerned with authenticity. It's guided by a higher value: user growth.

Rachel Ehmke of the Child Mind Institute breaks down Fortnite's addictive strategy to win over young users:

> Fortnite certainly isn't the first game to let people play together on a team. But Fortnite introduces younger kids to the adrenalin-inducing appeal of a first-person shooter game that is played in real time with friends. That's because parents are

more likely to give younger kids their blessing to play Fortnite, since its cartoon graphics aren't especially gruesome.[8]

What matters is that it *appears* to be better even if the format is just as addicting. Kayfabe.

The problem isn't that these media makers are mixing social interactive elements into these games. Games have always been inherently social and interactive whether they're digital or physical. The problem lies with their makers' intention to manipulate that social component, to strategically induce the fear of missing out, or to commoditize status, constantly incentivizing bigger and better. In plain daylight, companies are busy creating an economy that strategically causes kids to feel "less than" for being their ordinary selves outside of an imaginary world designed to generate profits. It's unnecessary inequity. Kids have a lifetime to contemplate what their economic status means. Why rob them of the innocence of not having to care what others think about the personal brands they've curated? Why rush them into forgetting the art of being an ordinary human being, something their freshness to the planet and lowness to the ground makes them so naturally good at?

If these kinds of games are the building blocks of the metaverse, is that the kind of world worth escaping this one for?

That weakness, the one all media makers have felt since the first story was told, that leads them to deliberately hide the truth from their audience as a form of domination, now has a name: gaslighting. But media that more transparently and deliberately uses the wonders of imagination, fantasy, and even illusion to lead people to arrive at the truth—that's art.

Picasso didn't pretend his surrealist, abstract figures were actually humans. He wielded the boundlessness of artistic expression in portraying the human body to draw us closer to the magnificence of our ordinary selves.

"Art is not truth," the Spanish master once said. "Art is a lie that makes us realize truth, at least the truth that is given us to understand."

Or consider Fred Rogers, who went to painstaking lengths to teach children the difference between ordinary life and the world of make-believe, at times even balking at the advanced media technology available to him. If any soul knew how to hold the beatitude of both worlds together, it was him.

How, then, do we become artists in a world where kay-fabe is king? How do we usher in a century where those to whom we're accountable see stories and meta-narratives as a pathway to love the parts of themselves still tethered to the earth?

The most important way to do this is to champion some of the more forgotten senses, especially touch.

The metaverse is limited by the senses it can conjure. Digital media will always be a two-fifths technology. Yes, we've expanded the horizon of what any of our ancestors could have fathomed when it comes to sight and sound, but have we forgotten the gratitude they must have felt for their other three gifts? Senses that can only be enhanced by the stuff of earth, conjured only by the labor of ordinary hands? These are not arbitrary remnants of nostalgia. They are mandatory for our survival.

Consider what happens, for instance, each time we choose to respond with a "thumbs up" emoji versus any other kind of acknowledgment. We are narrowing the sensory impulse, missing a multitude of sensory context. It's impossible to interpret meaning using a minimal data set like emojis or even brief text messages. We need more ordinary human contact.

Video screens and personal computers are useful and practical learning devices for students, but if we passively sway toward an education landscape where kids spend the majority of their time in front of screens, we won't teach them the communication nuances they desperately need to understand in order to peacefully coexist with other humans. This is why some among Generation Z have reported interpreting the "thumbs up" emoji as passive-aggressive whenever they receive it in a message from their employer.[9] When we lack sensory context, we make up our own.

Once you've eradicated nuance, once you've stripped communication of human intricacy, it makes brutality and tyranny easier to fester. You no longer have to be compassionate or conscientious; you can simply give a "thumbs up" to an avatar.

Any psychologist worth their salt knows our species can't survive without physical connection to each other. You might call touch the sacrament of the ordinary. It's mystery and mercy wrapped up in palpable participation. It continues to surprise me how little this fact seems to poke its head out to confront us amid our excitement for a growing metaverse.

My friend, Dr. Marc Mednick, is one of the most brilliant child psychotherapists I know. He explained the necessity of touch from a clinical perspective in a note to me that I'm publishing here with his permission:

> Infant research tells us that premature babies thrive more easily when touched. They gain weight faster, are generally more alert, and are easier to soothe and mold to you when picked up, as compared to preemies that are not touched as much. Touch—soothing, stroking, patting gently, are essential for early emotional attachments. Infants learn to associate smell with the touch of their nursing mother, along with the expectation that they will be fed.
>
> Oxytocin, a hormone, is released with nurturing touch, and is related to a general sense of well-being and increased social and emotional interest.
>
> It turns out that learning the reciprocity of touch is related to the development of strong social bonds, the development of compassion,

and the recognition of empathy. Without opportunities for touch, social bonds fray, and our neurobiological response tends to be one of withdrawal.

When people lose touch with touching, they tend to be more aggressive, cynical, and hostile. Without consistent, appropriate, nurturing touch in our social lives, our cognitive processing is divorced from an essential sensory input. Without social proximity, and without having to negotiate personal space, for example, our feelings towards each other are no longer mediated by the presence of another. No wonder the online climate can sometimes be so callous and unforgiving.

You may remember Ai Aoyama, the Japanese sex and relationship therapist, from a few chapters back. This is the bulk of her work—helping young men addicted to digital stimulation reconnect with the vastly superior pleasure of touching another human being. This, it seems, is the work before us, the art we must master for the sake of one another: to place the stories our eyes and ears can't escape back into their binding by reconnecting with the electricity that already courses through us.

Simply reacquainting ourselves with the eminence that is our mere physical presence alongside one another, the life-breathing, context-contributing energy such a mystery produces, would be medicinal in the age of the metaverse.

We Westerners have become more aware of the benefits personal meditation has to offer, but what about acts of *communal* meditation? Can they help us remember the forgotten art of being ordinary?

The Jewish tradition of sitting shiva, the act of comforting a family who has lost a loved one simply by sharing space with them, is communal meditation. When people sit shiva they make purposeful visits to each one of the senses. They embrace each other, tell each other stories about the one who's passed on, cook meals for each other, and, at times, perhaps most profoundly, sit in silence alongside those who are mourning. During those moments, there is no script, there is no performance, there is only nuance: subtle shades of meaning, expressions, and sounds.

Jazz is communal meditation, a nuance-saturated act of group creation and group listening, In jazz, there is no veil between personal brand and audience. Everyone is participating, whether their fingers are on an instrument, tapping lightly on the tablecloth, or pairing a sip to a sound in harmonious agreement. Jazz is the ritual of temporarily releasing our sense of individuality and control for a sense of collective uncertainty, an invitation to collaborative surprise. As the jazz trumpeter Wynton Marsalis mused, "Jazz music is the power of now. There is no script. It's conversation. The emotion is given to you by musicians as they make split-second decisions to fulfil what they feel the moment requires."[10]

Encouraging our kids (and each other) to rediscover these multisensory, nuance-heavy rituals—to garden, cook, improvise, hike, swim, and raise animals; to steep themselves in experiences where all five senses are directly linked to each other, tasting, smelling, and touching what they're also seeing and hearing, even when it's uncomfortable—just may save them from ejecting out of the miracle of ordinary life completely, even if that desire is admittedly justified at times.

Yes, we have significant problems here in actual reality: climate change, democracy under siege, rampant inequity. We keep pursuing fiction because it's easier than dealing with the facts. We opt into virtual worlds because we can't accept our current one.

We can teach our kids and, more importantly, model for them the reality that digital escapes from physical problems won't change the fact that those problems still exist. Nor will escaping remove their consequences. We won't repair the earth if we simply move on to something we think is better. Whether or not we're conscious of it, we are still very much tethered to what we're tempted to move on from. The opposite of integration is disintegration. If we forget to practice the sacrament of touch, if we fail to dig our hands back into the soil we've neglected, feel the rains rise up to our knees before they overwhelm us, taste the salt and breathe the incense of undisturbed collisions, or risk the bright exposure of our own nakedness in order to procreate, we won't just die, we'll disintegrate. *That's* reality.

In addition to championing the forgotten senses, we can start to become quiet rebels.

We can learn from my quiet friend David, whose sonic tangent began this chapter, and begin to construct better instrument cables, ones that cut down on the cacophony. We can recognize one of our greatest defenses against kayfabe is the voluntary steps we take to minimize the noise surrounding each other, the potentially unpopular eliminations we can make in order to liberate our voices to resonate in their purest, most real melody. We can acknowledge that the metal mechanics we now live with are necessary for conducting energy, connecting one thing to another, but also attract a tidal wave of "techno-ference" that directly inhibits the ordinary elegance inside us and around us from singing through. We can make choices that are sure to go against the masses, choices that uproot the dissonance, the buzz, the ferocious fiction in a sheep suit. We can name it for what it is so we know what we're looking for. We can risk the fear of missing out to discover the contagious elation of *opting* out. We can choose to do the difficult work of subtracting, insulating, and softening once in a while, if only to remember the forgotten art of being ordinary, the communion that accompanies flesh and blood.

How you go about that, what you choose to remove or taper, is up to you. For me, as you'll learn in the next chapter, I had to move to Westerville, Ohio—the nerve center of the failed Temperance Movement.

07

TEMPERANCE TOWN

Media in Moderation

LITTLE

We used to speak in person
Back before you bought that house with the HOA,
The brick one with the symmetrical arborvitaes.
I would come over, put the kettle on
And we'd talk in spindles without a care for sticks or
    stones.

Was it something I said?
A curse I put over our heads?
Now all you point out is the rain-rotting in my basement
And the holes that need to be thatched.

It was like that way for years—
Before the Wolf came
And heaved us all into close corners
too tight for text messages,
too converging for birthday cards.

All this time I thought
ours was a tale about siding.
Now, in the stillness of little things
I recognize it was about brotherhood.

Beatitude

05.

BLESSED ARE THOSE
WHO HUDDLE CLOSE,
FOR THEY SHALL BE
SET FREE.

In the fall of 2021, after nearly two years spent assessing our priorities and values—thrown into the naked light after the coronavirus forced us all deep into our own "roof and walls and fireplace"—my family and I decided to sell our home in Nashville and move to Columbus, Ohio. We did so for several reasons, a few of which I'll explain in this chapter. We landed in a neighborhood called Westerville, where it turned out my wife's ancestors, a family called the Hanbys, have ties. William Hanby founded Otterbein University, just about a mile away from us, and offered his family's modest house as a stop on the Underground Railroad. His son, a musician named Benjamin, wrote the antislavery ballad "My Darling Nelly Gray" as well as the Christmas tune "Up on the Housetop." Westerville is an old historic college town. What we didn't know is that more than a century ago, it became ground zero for America's famous fight against the "demon rum."

Indeed, Westerville was the home of the Anti-Saloon League, whose headquarters were what is now its Public Library, originally built around the league's 1893 debut. Their emphatic war against alcohol ultimately ended in temporary victory with the national enactment of Prohibition in 1920.

Initially headquartered in Washington, DC, the League switched its operations to Westerville in 1909 for a number of reasons, the biggest being media and technology. Here, the league could establish and run a proper printing center. Not only was Westerville close to Columbus, it also offered a railroad station advantageous for shipping and distributing print materials all over the country. These and the fact that business owners had donated land as an incentive made the migration from DC to Westerville most opportune.

The final reason the League ultimately chose Westerville is because the town had been dry since 1859. One member of the League bragged that the city was "so dry that you have to sprinkle the streets after a rain."

There was the occasional rebel. A man named Henry Corbin tried to open a saloon twice, in 1875 and then 1879. Both times the townspeople blew up his establishment using homemade bombs, one of which knocked two of Henry's teeth out. He tried opening for a third time, this time carrying a pistol in each hand to defend himself. He was bombed again and switched to selling vegetables.

Unsurprisingly, the Anti-Saloon League found a supportive atmosphere in Westerville. A blurb from Ohio's *Beacon Journal* expands:

> Here it could tread the moral high ground, researching the physical and emotional effects of drinking, keeping tabs on liquor laws around the country and cranking out posters, paycheck inserts, children's stories and other materials aimed at turning America against alcohol—40 tons' worth of printed material a month in its peak years.
>
> "Do you know? One insane person in every four owes his insanity to drink," trumpets one of the league's fliers on display in the museum.
>
> Another depicts a child alone in a squalid home on Christmas Eve while Dad tosses back drinks in a bar.
>
> There are buttons declaring "Bread Not Booze," posters decrying the evils of liquor and copies of the American Issue, the league's anti-alcohol newspaper. The league also published a number of books, including an annual yearbook on the progress of the liquor issue and the Standard Encyclopedia of the Alcohol Problem, an ambitious compendium of alcohol and liquor-law information collected by editor Ernest Cherrington.[1]

Sounding over the top to our twenty-first-century sensibilities, today these anti-alcohol messages might deserve a soundtrack written by Sarah McLachlan. However, the problems the league was addressing were objectively serious. The growing nation had a shortage of clean water, directly increasing the use (and abuse) of alcohol, all amid a society where women had little autonomy, facing abuse and destitution if their husbands decided to drink away their paychecks (which many did)[2]—a main reason why the Temperance Movement and the women's suffrage movement were so interconnected.

That era's cultural relationship with alcohol, something not entirely bad but very much lacking boundaries, became a growing problem that happened to carry with it several interconnected causes, all of which had a marked effect on the entire family unit, leading to several needed shifts in our democratic policy and cultural worldview. Does that remind you of any other time?

As public opinion turned against Prohibition, the league likewise fell in esteem. After Repeal in 1933, the Anti-Saloon League began a terminal decline. Westerville, however, would remain dry until 2004, when a pub called the Old Bag of Nails threw the dice and applied for a liquor license, hoping people's reactions had tempered since the 1800s and no teeth would be lost in the process:

As it turned out, voters by an overwhelming margin—71 percent—approved the license for the Old Bag of Nails pub. Before the pub could be renovated and opened, though, Michael's Pizza got a liquor license, too. It was there, on Jan. 12, 2006, that the first beer since 1933 (a Budweiser) was served Uptown.[3]

The shift awakened the laden potential of this small, historic blip of a college town. Tony Cabilovsk, the owner of one of my favorite local watering holes, affectionately named Temperance Brewing, recalls a different kind of Westerville than the one he knows today. "Ten years ago, if you went through Westerville at 8 PM on a Tuesday, it was a ghost town. Now it's vibrant, and it's not just the restaurants and bars that are full, it's the boutiques and shops, as well."

By the way, not long after Tony opened in 2015, a decedent of Henry Corbin stopped in to say thanks for succeeding where his ancestor had tried in vain. If you ever visit, look me up and we'll get a couple of beers from Temperance named in Henry's honor: "Corbin's Revenge" and "Two Pistols."[4]

Outside of Westerville City Hall, there's now a sculpture of a broken whiskey barrel. The town plumbed it with water so it looks like it's spilling out the sides, an homage to what Westerville once fought for, and a celebration of what it no longer needed to.

I go back and forth on which side of Prohibition I would have found myself. Given some of the reasoning behind the desire to deny alcohol to the public, it's also easy to conjure empathy for those fighting for a ban on something that had gotten out of control. Alcohol wasn't the reason women were disempowered or children left vulnerable, but its toxicity, when used without discretion or foresight, worsened many of the inequitable problems already facing the culture. Again, stop me when you've heard this one.

But in a much larger way, the whole thing sounds archaic, myopic, and hypermoralistic. The evidence that the amendment caused more harm than good is overwhelming. Prohibition was ultimately ineffective when strictly enforced from the top down. Yes, there were bad actors and ignorant practices when it came to producing and selling alcohol, but there were also immigrants who, over thousands of years in the regions that became Germany, had perfected the slow process of crafting excellent, low-ABV beer. Prohibition blacklisted them both. In the end, the need to climb from the depths of the Great Depression made Prohibition too costly a battle, and its legacy a failure to accomplish what it set out to do.

Around 1935, two years after Prohibition's repeal, another movement began percolating just about ninety minutes north of Westerville in Akron, Ohio. A man named Bill Wilson, who had been struggling with alcoholism his entire adult life and had been in and out of rehabilitation programs, had just come to Ohio for a business trip. The deal ended up falling through and the entire journey was looking like yet another personal failure, one more piled atop a crushing heap of them. Tempted to run to the nearest local bar, Wilson, in a moment of lucidity, came up with a Hail Mary idea. He needed to find another alcoholic. Perhaps focusing on helping someone else stay sober would steer his attention toward a solution more fulfilling than cheap whiskey.

He got his hands on a local church directory and began randomly calling numbers. I'd love to know how those conversations went.

"Are you an alcoholic?

"No?

"All right, know anyone who is? . . . Hello?"

Finally, Bill found Bob Smith. The two began meeting, sharing stories, helping each other through their darkest memories, and encouraging each other when temptation knocked at their door. It worked. A failed business trip to Akron successfully birthed Alcoholics Anonymous, a program Bill and Bob centered around small, intimate gatherings of people sharing the story of their addiction with each other, acknowledging their intention to quit, and agreeing to call each other if tempted to backslide. Nearly a century since its inception, many see AA as one of the most effective methods for treating alcoholism.

The architecture of the Alcoholics Anonymous network is fascinating. Local AA groups are products of spontaneous order, people assembling without any significant hierarchy or institution pulling the strings. Instead, there are guiding principles, or traditions, shared and valued among participants centered around this idea of ordinariness, one of them being the suggestion that members remain anonymous when speaking to public media, and that no one use the group for their own personal financial gain or celebrity.

It's as if the intimate infrastructure Bill and Bob designed held a mirror to the Prohibition movement and replied, "*This* is how you change a culture, not by public shame and sweeping regulation, but one soul at a time, in the company of a few fellow ordinary humans, holding nothing more but each other in the fragile solidarity of hope."

It's the reason we moved.

Back to Temperance Town and why we decided to make it our home: Apart from Westerville reorienting its attention from championing Prohibition to investing in incredible public spaces—libraries, parks, schools, and bike paths—one of the central reasons we migrated there was a longing for that sense of solidarity, a genuine feeling of community and neighborhood we had been lacking. Two more reasons were our friends John and Erin.

Of all the places in the world, I met John and Erin on an old farm Johnny Cash used to own. We were all living in Nashville at the time and had been invited by a wealthy, eccentric old man who had recently bought the sprawling property in Bon Aqua, Tennessee. We traversed the acreage, stomping through the muddy grass, avoiding cow pies and strange looks from curious locals, to help the mysterious old man envision what he might do with the place now that he owned it. The conversation never really went anywhere con-sequential (I'm not even sure if he still owns the place), but it was one of those strange, serendipitous encounters, meet-ing the folks who would become some of your best friends on a parcel where an American storytelling giant once ate, slept, worked, and played. Was the ghost of Johnny Cash still presiding over his old haunts, still making stories and stringing together unlikely harmonies? Was he upset that I had used his heated toilet seat?

John and Erin had a daughter just a few years older than ours. All of us just seemed to click: John with me; Erin with my wife, Kelly; and their daughter, Lilly, with our daughter, Selah. Rare, right? Anyone in a serious relationship with a partner will know what I mean when I say that the odds of making compatible friendships get cut in half once you decide to double up your life with someone else. Add kids to that equation and it becomes exponentially harder!

There was something else that my wife and I had in common with John and Erin. We were all trying to practice some intentionality when it came to raising our kids in the age of the Great Distraction, a similarity that turned out to be remarkably helpful. Being aligned with other parents who didn't want the next generation to fuse so singularly with their technological devices that they forgot the beauty of their ordinary, untethered selves helped shape how both of our kids played together. There wasn't an excessive fear of missing out because Selah had Lilly and Lilly had Selah.

I remember the day, a little over a year after that ghostly encounter on the farm, when John told me they'd decided to move back to Columbus to be closer to aging family. My heart sank and yet I knew somehow this wasn't the end. There was still another verse to this song. It just needed a bridge.

After they moved, we visited each other frequently in order to keep spending time together. Every time we visited them in Columbus, I felt more and more like it was a city where I could imagine us raising our kids. There's an international and immigrant influence that reminded me of growing up in New York, the kind that produces a diversity in everything—food, music, culture, politics.

I had missed that in the insulated little suburb where we'd settled outside of Nashville. Sure, it was beautiful, but everything was homogeneous, which made me wonder if I was confusing actual beauty with a script about such things. Maybe I had kayfabed myself.

I wanted my kids to grow up normalizing diversity and gaining a more sophisticated understanding of our storied, multifaceted history, full of collaborative triumph and collective failures. Especially once the 2020s rolled around, it seemed like many Southerners were doubling down on some old narratives, ensuring we kept teaching our kids "alternative facts."

Most importantly, I wanted to live among a fellowship of friends with similar values when it came to the parents we wanted to be, the kinds of kids we wanted to raise, and the communities we wanted to shape. We moved to Westerville, Ohio, of all places, to find ourselves among a small circle of companions who were rejecting the lure of personal branding and media addiction for a life centered around each other, the prevailing gifts of ordinary work and play, of the simple principles and traditions our families would thrive under, especially our kids.

It's one thing to attempt those traditions or try to mandate them. It's another thing to practice them in community alongside others. This is what Bill and Bob understood that the Temperance Movement didn't.

The other morning, I walked to the local Westerville doughnut shop, where I overheard a mom pleading with her ten- or eleven-year-old boy to put down his phone and join the moment. You and I have heard this exchange thousands of times. We've even identified with this poor mom just trying to do the right thing. This resulted in the typical eye rolls and power struggle as it framed the conversation around what the boy would rather do versus what he "ought to do" (even if that wasn't his mom's intent).

Turning down the noise, becoming better cables for each other (as we discussed in the last chapter), doesn't imply simply trusting your ten-year-old with a privacy-sucking machine and occasionally monitoring screen time when you feel it's appropriate. That's a strategy we can all agree isn't working. There needs to be another step, a greater intentionality worth exploring, one that's more concerned with seeking out community than making compromises.

Once we found our people, it became easier to create a family rhythm that allowed for the use of media technology without succumbing to the Great Distraction.

To be clear, I am not advocating we all go about creating enclaves of Luddite children with no sense of media literacy. Our little Columbus kid collective watches movies and TV shows together on occasion. They also ride their bikes, play hide and seek, and make lemonade stands.

More importantly, I'm not suggesting you need to move somewhere different from where you already find yourself. My aim is to simply pose a question I had to ask myself at some point, a question every addict, be it to alcohol or media, must ask: What people will remind you of your ordinariness and love you for it? What will you do to seek them out and make sure they're never far? What step of courage and discomfort may be necessary to find solidarity and support amid a culture that praises rugged individualism and autonomy?

Finally, I realize how remarkably lonely life can feel in our modern era of pseudo relationships gated by screens and devices. The community and belonging you long for may seem impossible to access; while media technology, on the other hand, is faithful as the day is long. I'm struck by Bill Wilson's tenacity in finding Bob Smith, combing through the church directory, talking to anyone who'd pick up the phone. Without trivializing the difficulty of what I'm about to suggest, perhaps lean into the awkwardness of making your ordinary presence known. Fight to be sought out, seen, and listened to by seeking out, seeing, and listening to your fellow earthly travelers. When the impulse comes to post a political opinion online, search for the nearest volunteer opportunity. Join a club in the wake of joining a chatroom. Invest in an exercise group that meets down the street instead of purchasing a Peloton bike. Step across the rickety threshold of your own incarnation to find the very same desires you have in those who share a common sky.

None of us will live to see a prohibition of media technology and all its anxiety-producing consequences. Nor should it be prohibited. We've been down that road before. It would be difficult to restrict the bad without eliminating all the good this technology has produced. What we *can* do is find each other, rekindle the abandoned sacrament of neighborhood, and see us as the common siblings we once were, before the Great Distraction.

Worth noting, these relationships do not have to align completely with each other or always agree on best practices. When it comes to our little Columbus community, we're all simply doing the research, making the best educated guesses we can, and trying to deliver what we think our kids uniquely need from us. I've come to enjoy dialoguing with John and mutual friends about what works for their kids versus mine, what is turning out to be helpful versus what's backfiring, how their thoughts and opinions are changing as their kids grow older, and how to navigate the fact that my wife and I may land at different conclusions at different points for our own.

If that sounds like a lot of work, it can be. Occasional discomfort is the currency that subsidizes genuine community. Try as some may, you cannot automate away the human desire for human relationship. To make matters a bit more complicated, you and I know quite well that our capacity for that particular flavor of nuanced long-form communication has been challenged, conditioned out of us by an overreliance on the very devices we are trying to limit, not to mention nearly two years spent in isolation warding off a global pandemic.

In fact, for all the societal catching up we are now having to do after March 2020 forced us into near isolation, perhaps one aspect we can retain as we come out of the depths of the pandemic is the emergence of localized "pods" or "clusters": groups of families who agreed to limit social interactions to each other so they could at least spend time in physical proximity, enjoying the natural, grounded world around them, cooking, eating, connecting in all three dimensions, reveling in the awkward reawakening of all five senses. As horrible as the coronavirus has been for countless people around the world, for all the physical, emotional, and financial struggle it continues to cause, for me the global pandemic paradoxically also became a time of great healing, a reconnecting with what's most important, closest, and present; a necessary inward correction, a darkening that turned what was light into a laser.

It turns out that close, compact networks are the remedy for ones that depend solely on the loose slack of somewhat-social media. They produce the kind of connectivity that is the antithesis of a pseudo-anonymous online back-and-forth or reality-blurring competition in the metaverse. It's not attention seeking but empathy sharing. It's what we'll refer to in the next chapter as "a collective journey."

08

THE HERO IS DEAD

Media as Collective Journey

1 AM OUTSIDE METROPOLIS

"What an interesting thing, to get over ourselves,"
said Clark to Bruce.

The two were hunched under the dim bar lights.
Clark cupped his usual Pabst
while Bruce raced cherries around his Manhattan.

"That secret identity, the one I hid—
It was more like being naked inside a phone booth."

Bruce chewed a sip and swallowed.
"At least you weren't dumb enough to do the mask thing.
ZERO peripheral vision.
All my hits came sideways."

Clark took a final swig and raised his finger at the bartender.
"I tripped on my cape a couple of times."

"Oh, me too. Always made them edit that out."

Removing his glasses, Clark rubbed the bridge of his nose.
"Hey, where'd you go, buddy?" cracked Bruce.

Reapplying them, he swept his cowlick and mumbled,
"I almost forgot what it's like to feel my feet on the ground."

Bruce scratched the shadow off his chin and let some air escape
his nostrils.
"Kind of like coming out of a cave."

Beatitude

06.

BLESSED ARE THOSE WHO TELL NEW STORIES, FOR THEY SHALL BE CALLED PEACEMAKERS OF THE TWENTY-FIRST CENTURY.

At twenty-four years old, Ahmed was convinced he had landed the role of a lifetime. He'd already been a successful jazz musician and was currently performing in the hit show *Stomp* on Broadway. Not many artists his age could say that. This new role, however, was what you'd call a next-level gig. A few nights earlier, a casting director was sitting in the audience of *Stomp*. He was looking for actors to star in George Lucas's long-anticipated prequel to his blockbuster Star Wars trilogy.

Two years later, at the turn of the twenty-first century, *Star Wars: The Phantom Menace* came out. The reception from critics and fans to Ahmed's role, a CGI-enhanced character named Jar Jar Binks, was almost unanimously negative.

Remember, 1999 saw the spreading kayfabe of reality TV coupled with some of the first public internet message boards and editorial-page comment sections—digital "third spaces" where fans could find each other and exchange viewpoints. That experience alone may have felt somewhat like a video game to people, a sphere where words couldn't possibly have the same amount of power they do in person simply because they were faceless, transmitted electronically over a medium still unknown and indecipherable to many.

I believe we can draw a direct line back to this point, the one being toed by Generation Z (whose earliest members were born around this time), which emphasizes the notion that words can in fact equal violence. It's a correction, if sometimes an extreme one, of the lack of understanding and regard for the fact that ideas and attacks transmitted digitally can have real-world, physical consequences.

They did for Ahmed. Ahmed Best, who played Jar Jar Binks in the 2002 and 2005 Star Wars prequels, feared his very life was in danger over those burgeoning digital transmission lines.

"I had death threats through the internet," recalled Ahmed in a 2017 *Wired* interview. "I had people come to me and say, 'You destroyed my childhood.' That's difficult for a 25-year-old to hear."[1]

One aspect of the turn-of-the-century reality TV boom we haven't discussed yet, but which I think has relevance, is how producers began to experiment with emerging interactive consumer potential. As internet and mobile technologies were advancing, and as media became smaller, more accessible, and ever closer to the audiences' fingertips, networks naturally looked for ways to capture and capitalize on that widening sea of available data. Contest-driven reality shows like *American Idol* and *The X Factor* began experimenting with letting audiences vote on which contestants they liked best—a primitive precursor to the modern "like" button. Audiences now had a direct say in the outcome of a story, as participants, not spectators. Is it so wide a stretch to suspect that such newfound agency and investment, combined with an equally newfound blurring of lines between reality and fiction, began to produce a generation of fans more prone to confusing an actor with the character they play, to the point where they would feel licensed and compelled to personally attack them?

If that's feasible, then perhaps another, more hopeful possibility awaits us as well. In the age of hyperinteractivity, where everyone is now irrevocably intertwined as stakeholders in the stories our culture tells, could we potentially leverage this burden with both wisdom and thoughtfulness to shape stories that produce empathy and connectivity, that press into the wonder of our ordinary humanity, rather than *de*humanize us?

We can keep using our newfound agency as story participants to further bolster kayfabe, obscuring the divide between reality and performance, or we can use it to collectively change the kinds of stories we tell altogether, ones that live in the future we hope for, not the past. We can begin telling each other different narratives than the ones we've been relying on for centuries, tropes designed for a more individualistic culture where there was one distinct hero and an equally distinct villain.

In the classic "hero's journey," we, the audience, root for hypercurated versions of what's right and wrong, then relax and watch the conflict play out. Today, though, what worked for centuries around the campfire and in theatres with floor-to-ceiling projections doesn't fit our modern multichannel, democratized, pocket-sized media palette. For the first time in our history, we've created a completely accessible and interactive ecosystem where we no longer perceive a line between audience and storyteller, consumer and creator.

That evolution has gotten ahead of our storytelling sensibilities. In many ways, we're still campfire people living in a decentralized metaverse, and our kneejerk response to perpetuate the same old storylines we've always known demonstrates that. To make matters more complex, as media technology has advanced to the point where we now all have access to our own mini storytelling studios, we have tended to become our own hypercurated characters, placing ourselves in the role of "hero" in search of a "villain" to destroy, a wrong to make right, and a village to champion our conquest.

We all can't be heroes, though. Just as Ahmed is not Jar Jar, we are not characters. We're ordinary, flawed, complicated humans. The hero's journey, it turns out, doesn't scale very well in the twenty-first century.

In an era of perpetual media, of constant reboots and ongoing franchises, there are only so many times Luke

Skywalker can defeat the Empire before we start to question *why* the Empire continues to be a threat. There are only so many times a politician can promise that they're the one who can make things better before we question why the system keeps failing us. There's only so much trust we can give our cultural heroes to fix life's problems before it emerges that those heroes actually contributed to those problems behind the scenes.

The old hero's story is getting worn out. It puts too much weight on the few without recognizing the latent potential of the many, what my friend Jeff Gomez calls a "collective journey."[2]

Jeff grew up a Puerto Rican kid on the streets of New York City. He was in and out of the foster system, and describes his childhood as haunted by poverty, chaos, and shame. What he may have lacked in privilege, he made up for in scrappiness, along with the cosmic guidance of misfit angels: the superheroes he revered and read about in comic books.

Today, he pays homage to the mythos that guarded his imagination by consulting for some of the world's largest and most prolific entertainment studios, corporations, and even governments on how to tell new types of stories that capture twenty-first-century sensibilities. The entertainment company he heads, affectionately called Starlight Runner, has run projects ranging from helping Marvel and Sony Studios bridge their separate Spider-Man multiverses (eventually culminating in the movies like *Captain America: Civil War* and *Spider-Man: No Way Home*) to helping the fledgling Colombian government navigate their youth crisis after years of civil unrest.

For years, Jeff has been methodically writing and teaching about this shift from leaning heavily on the hero's-journey modality toward embracing a collective-journey mindset. When I met with him to discuss the role collective journeys could play in helping us harness the metaverse without losing our soul, his fidelity to the concept showed.

From Jeff's perspective, throughout history, popular storytelling seems to cycle through five distinct genre stages:

> The evolution of genre in storytelling always starts off as Experimental. This is where we're just beginning to think about some new way of telling a story. Then there's the Classic era, where you're done working out the kinks, get the story down right, and everyone loves it. Phase three is Refinement, where the story gets really good, critically pristine. The fourth phase is Baroque, meaning things start to get strange and reflexive. You begin talking about the story *in* the story. Stuff starts doubling. Finally, there's Deconstruction. This is where you start to smash the story. The story criticizes itself by taking itself apart.

I understood what Jeff was saying on a macro level, but just to make sure we were on the same page, I asked him to cite a few examples.

Let's look at the Universal Monsters franchise. The Experimental phase was *Phantom of the Opera* all the way back in the 1920s. That was so strange and weird for that time with Lon Chaney in all that makeup. Then there was the Classic phase with films like *Dracula, Frankenstein*, and *The Mummy.* The Refinement phase was *Bride of Frankenstein*, which is truly a great movie. The Baroque phase would be *Frankenstein Meets the Wolf Man* where they're starting to do these weird crossovers. Finally, Deconstruction looked like *Abbott and Costello Meet Frankenstein*. Later, other studios would create shows like *The Addams Family* and *The Munsters*. As an audience we're not scared anymore, we're laughing.

Here's a more recent example, Marvel. The Experimental phase in the Marvel Cinematic Universe was *Hulk* and *Iron Man*. In those first two movies, they didn't quite know exactly what they were doing, but it suggested something that was going to be awesome. The Classic phase is *Captain America* and *The Avengers*. The Refinement phase would be *Winter Soldier* and *Guardians of the Galaxy*. That's where they really started to present themselves as excellent films executed with great confidence. The Baroque phase would be *Deadpool, WandaVision,* and *Spider-Man 3*. There are doubles and variants, a kind of bending and twisting of plots and concepts. We haven't really gotten to the Deconstruction phase with Marvel yet, but a helpful equivalent would be DC's *Watchmen* or the SnyderVerse.

I understood this cycle now, how our most ubiquitous cultural narratives iterate and transition over time once they become stale. But if that same cycle has been repeating for centuries, what did it have to do with this newfound sense of autonomy we have as fellow storytellers now intimately involved in the story-creation process?

Jeff believes that, just as all popular narrative genres go through this five-stage cycle, the broader culture experiences these stage shifts as well. He believes we're currently in the Baroque phase of our own "supernarrative," well on the way to Deconstruction. We're diluting and mocking ourselves. Our continuity is unraveling. We're recasting. Reality stars are ruling the free world. Teenage girls live in mansions designed for television. Discerning what is real from what has been fabricated is no longer simple. It's kayfabe. And it's exhausting.

That's where the *reconstructive* model of the collective journey presents itself as a welcome alternative. As Jeff notes:

Collective journey presents a modality that is different. If each of us is a hero running through the hero's journey cycle, going out into the world, defeating anything that gets in our way, retrieving food or fire and bringing it back to the community so that we can thrive, this cycle is hardwired into our minds and with that comes the compelling necessity of asserting our rightness on the wrongness of others.

With collective journey, we are stepping back from that. I am not denying that hero's journey is hardwired. I am saying we are now smart enough to say, "because we are interconnected with each other, it's no longer productive to us to continue retracing these simplistic circles." If we step back far enough, we can see a system that is so flawed, so damaged that if we don't do something about it collectively, it will destroy us—ALL of us—whether we are gaining from the system or losing from it.

What exactly does a collective-journey narrative look like? While they often still feature a main character whose point of view leads the story, we also see that story world and the issues at hand through multiple perspectives. Collective-journey narratives are more about the interplay between a group of interconnected characters across a flawed system than the battle between a hero and a villain. Some are thriving from those flaws. Others work in service of them. Still others are suffering because of these flaws. The most important aspect to understand is that collective journey is not about individualistic defeat and conquest. It's about the interplay of characters across this system to address the flaws. The solutions lie not in confrontations between good and evil, but in the juxtaposition of perspectives. They resolve themselves through what Jeff calls "the drama of reconciliation." He provided two of his favorite examples:

> There are two stories in current circulation which have become wildly popular: *Encanto* and *Ted Lasso*. Although they're entirely different visually and rooted in two different cultures, there's a lot they have in common. These are two universes, two systems that have flaws in them. And what they *do not* do is point the finger at a villain. Instead, the characters in both stories slowly start to realize that the flaw in the system is being perpetuated by trauma, negative emotions, events, and situations that have occurred in the past and get passed down, not even exclusively from a parent to a child, but multi-generationally, perhaps even in the distant past—perceptions, biases, faux pas.

This is quite a different response to negative characters than the archetypal "you're going to have to be killed (or at least be banished) in order for us to achieve some kind of resolution" response. Jeff continues:

There is no good and evil in collective journey, though some people can do terrible things in their own self-interest. Instead, we are presented with a story world where the reality of the situation is perceived across a spectrum of interpretations and the resolution emerges out of the dynamics of reconciliation. Climactic battles may still play out, but far more important in terms of story is the cleverness with which true and lasting systemic change is actualized. That's the kind of storytelling the world currently needs.

You've probably already connected the dots. Collective journey stories have a total meta component to them. They mirror our hyperdigital, hyperconnected world, in which we are all participants, fellow sojourners contributing to the kinds of entertainment narratives we imagine and hope for. But more than that, collective-journey stories deconstruct the kayfabe myths that no longer serve the well-being of the collective. The more we can pollinate these types of stories among ourselves, the more we can instill them in our kids, the more hope we have of creating a metaverse with a sense of minimum viable morality, something we all create, share, and hopefully agree on.

It's going to take a while," says Jeff. "Metaverse games like Fortnite and Minecraft are still predominately conflict oriented. They're 'hero's journey.' We have to enter into these things with a new mindset. Once we have a more collective journey mindset, these worlds can then be redesigned to take advantage of that and enhance it. But first we must change our minds."

Perhaps the spark of such a mind shift is hidden beneath another interesting trait of collective journey narratives. Stories like *Encanto, Turning Red*, and even more adult-oriented examples such as *Schitt's Creek* or *Only Murders in the Building* often achieve their arc not by shaming or shunning those who have perpetuated systemic myths but by offering discovery, insight, and opportunities to learn and grow.

As we've already discussed, it's become ever harder for a disembodied, disintegrated generation endlessly spun around by kayfabe to differentiate words and violence, a pendulum swing away from the mindset of digital immigrants who lacked any reverence for and restraint from the power and repercussions their online actions could have.

Jeff and I are hopeful that a move toward a collective-journey mindset could create a pathway to something beyond cancel culture, a movement toward reconciliation. Perhaps we can start to generate a greater understanding of the trauma operating *behind* the negative rhetoric we encounter in a metaverse dominated by a limited data set of symbols. Perhaps doing so will start to discharge their overemphasized power, which has tangled so many in knots and absorbed so much of our current media-driven ecosystem. There's hope in deconstructing while the worst of the metaverse fights to divide us further. From Jeff's perspective,

it's not going away. It's only going to intensify.
We need to be able to come to terms with our
[hypercurated] selves, the entire set of roles
that we take on in digital space, which can be
so alluring that it sucks us out of our physical
bodies, literally disembodying us.

That's why we need to encourage our kids to
start deconstructing, to be able to recognize the
underlying emotion behind charged language
and ask, "What happened to you? What is the
mechanism behind this?" We need to educate
them to stop being offended by the word and
start understanding where it's coming from.

Jeff ended our conversation with a stirring and sobering
speech reminiscent of a captain aboard a starship, piloting
from a galaxy far beyond our current meta-qualms:

By using the collective journey model, I'm going
to communicate to you from a future where we're
friends, no matter what you're saying to me right
now, no matter how horrific your language is. I
am speaking to you from a future where we are
allies. That mentality disarms the power of any
language that's being thrown at me and makes
me better able to reach and reconcile with the
person wielding those words. That could mean
the difference between war and peace.

Such a message may seem like mere stargazing, especially when you consider what Ahmed Best went through after portraying Jar Jar Binks. Is it not *the* message worth innovating, educating, and striving toward, though? Would it not deliver the outcomes we desire for all members of the collective involved: empowerment of the marginalized and reconciliation of those perpetuating flawed systems?

I believe so. And if the medium is still the message, then we have a lot of work to do.

On July 3, 2018, Ahmed posted a picture on the internet of himself and his son staring out over a bridge. The caption read, "20 years ago next year I faced a media backlash that still affects my career today. This was the place I almost ended my life. It's still hard to talk about. I survived and now this little guy is my gift for survival. Would this be a good story for my solo show? Lemme know."

Perhaps not a solo show, but an ensemble.

A post-script

In Spring 2023 as I was wrapping up the final edits of this book, the producers of the hit Star Wars TV series *The Mandalorian* surprised audiences around the world. They debuted an episode featuring Ahmed Best as a Jedi Knight, the most honored and revered archetype in the franchise's universe, and made him responsible for saving the series' most central and beloved character. Older fans understood the rhyme, the past mistreatment metamorphosed into honor, and enlightened younger fans on the journey that brought Ahmed to this point. These are the kinds of stories each of us is tasked with telling a new generation, stories where reconciliation is not simply a performance but something we practice together, no longer just a myth but a movement.

09

WHAT TO DO WITH LIL MIQUELA

Media as Mythology

ST. CHRISTOPHER

(For Aaron Flores and Steve Zeringue)

You are not a story
the rewrite is still too rickety
the overall genre still uncertain

No, you are a bridge
constructed by others
plunging stone into water
connecting cables to clouds

In the sureness of your own footing
stretch yourself across
where good men once drowned
as an act of gratitude and grace

It once took the healing hands of friends
to help me recognize
the mythology of my own greatness

Beatitude

07.

However worth it, the fight to view our journey into the metaverse as a col-lective one won't be simple. The hero's journey is still stuck deep in our ancestral genetics, continually siphoning us all into the roles of hero, villain, god, or scapegoat. How we parse these roles in the metaverse, whether we choose to redefine them, reimagine them, or scrap them all together, is something between an experiment and an arms race.

A headline that recently came across my screen had me raising an eyebrow and sent me down a rabbit hole. The California-based teen-clothing retailer PacSun had announced a partnership with what they were calling a "virtual influencer" named Lil Miquela as part of their strategy to build out their brand in the metaverse. At first I was tempted to dismiss this story as marketing nonsense from a mall brand struggling

BLESSED ARE THOSE
WHO LET GO OF
OLD MYTHS IN THE
METAVERSE, FOR
THEY SHALL FIND NEW
MEANING IN THE REAL
WORLD.

for relevancy in the age of e-commerce, but then I noticed that Lil Miquela (remember: *not* a real person) boasts over three million followers online! Full of questions and an unsettling feeling, I couldn't help but start my rabbit hole descent.

It turns out Lil Miquela is the creation of a company called Brud (which seems like a clever misspelling of the word "bread," meant as a colloquialism for money, especially when you consider their slogan, "Create worlds. Design narratives. Make brud.") They call themselves a Web 3.0 transmedia storytelling studio. Due almost entirely to the success of Lil Miquela, Brud's estimated market value exceeds $125 million.

The PacSun partnership isn't Lil Miquela's first robot rodeo. In the past several years, the hypercurated creation has partnered with the likes of Prada, Dior, and Calvin Klein.

Essentially, Lil Miquela is a semirealistic (though you can tell she's not a human), computer-generated character who, through artificial intelligence and superimposing, is made to look like she's interacting with the real world across web platforms that teenagers and young adults frequent. Photos taken of celebrities have been doctored later to appear as if they've taken a selfie with Lil Miquela. She also has a reputation for "showing up" at the latest trendy L.A. club or fashion event.

Nicole de Ayora, Brud's current chief content officer and a former celebrity gossip writer, allows us a few insights, however enigmatic, into their philosophy when it comes to Lil Miquela, via a video posted on Brud's website:

So ten years ago, I worked as a celebrity gossip blogger. It was an insane time to be a celebrity. But around that time, I was at a party where someone compared being a celebrity at that time to being a modern mythological god. The Britneys and the Lindsay Lohans—they get all this fame, they get all this fortune, and then all of a sudden they're thrust back into the human world, right? With the rest of us. And their strengths and their weaknesses basically lead to the development of new mythologies that are full of triumphs and failures.

. . . In a way, I see Miquela similarly as a distant relative of Roman mythology and a character that can potentially help carry that torch of such thought-provoking and allegorical narrative into new spaces. Her world is Los Angeles, but really her life is purely digital and has infinite potential within the boundlessness of the metaverse . . . She's a robot walking among humans . . . Her own code base and story have, at times, polarizing qualities but also incredible potential to ask larger questions and provide opportunities for people to learn from her life and help shape and challenge their opinions and values in the process.[1]

On the one hand, Brud's endeavor seems quite noble. Perhaps, at the very root of this conversation you and I have been having throughout this book, our tragic flaw as a society is the act of taking ordinary, everyday people and deifying them as larger than life.

But while Brud's chief content officer's summation of celebrity is close, I think it's one crucial degree off. It's a simple deviation, but it's the difference between using a prop like Lil Miquela to change our culture for the better or perpetuating a false narrative, perhaps making that narrative even worse.

Yes, celebrities *are* mythic. But our modern-day influencers aren't gods. We may call them idols, but it's for a different reason. We don't sacrifice *to* celebrities. They're actually *who* we wind up sacrificing. Celebrities are scapegoats.

For decades now, human remains once offered as scapegoats and sacrifices have been found in connection to the Aztec, Inca, Maya, and Moche cultures. Many of these remains are those of women and children. The Bible also makes references to child sacrifice, and there is evidence of it having been practiced in ancient Phoenicia and Carthage, Arabia, Europe, and Africa.

What is our ancient obsession with scapegoating? Why does it seem as baked into our genetics as the hero's journey? And why, as I'll explain, can't we seem to get away from mimicking this barbaric act even in the metaverse?

The late anthropologist René Girard believed this sacrificial pattern is at the root of all our mythmaking, tracing it all the way back to the earliest texts in history and even earlier. It was most likely the way we evolved and distinguished ourselves by creating distinct group identities before any of those texts were ever written, helping us string the very first strands of culture together.

According to Girard's analysis—what he calls "mimetic theory"—all conflict derives from humankind's desire for whatever their neighbor has. In other words, the reason we want something is because someone else wants it. Our natural inclination is to mimic our fellow humans, a practice that works well until two or more humans happen to desire the same scarce object—a recipe for conflict. Obviously, objects of desire are *most* scarce in times of chaos, suffering, and unrest, be it plague, economic crises, or wars. During these times the playing field gets leveled as everyone in the community suddenly becomes one another's rival.[2]

This ultimately gives way to "a sacrificial crisis." When a sacrificial crisis occurs, the community steeped in conflict creates a myth. They choose a scapegoat or "emissary victim," a third party around whom they can formulate a narrative that blames *them* for the crisis. This allows the community in conflict to turn their attack toward this victim instead of each other. According to Girard, "At some point, people must have been reconciled in order to create permanent communities, against not a leader directly, but a scapegoat that they kill together. The sacrifice serves to protect the entire community from its own violence."[3]

Scapegoat victims often possess some distinguishing characteristic that differentiates them from the other community members so they can be singled out. This is why throughout history, when it comes to sacrifices made by myth-driven cultures, they are commonly a child or virgin. A scapegoat must be special, separate, set apart—something that is often celebrated, cherished, even idolized—before it is eventually turned on and made to suffer.

Critics of Girard's theories have downplayed the idea that this pattern continues today in modern Western society. Yet the human tendencies that have played out across an ever-expanding metaverse throughout the twenty-first century make me think otherwise. We may not go around murdering adolescents in this millennium to solve our problems (as I write that, I can think of multiple instances where even that's debatable), but instead we simply prop up someone who doesn't fit the average stereotype, someone young and attractive who we hypercurate and design strategies around, someone who seems somehow exceptional but in actuality is a naturally fallible, ordinary person. Once these icons fall from perfection, we parade them around as a symbol for what happens when one flies too close to the sun. Brud mentioned Brittney Spears and Lindsay Lohan as examples. Justin Bieber and Logan Paul also come to mind, along with countless others.

The modern professional sports industry, led by corporations backed by shareholders, is yet another example of how our culture sacrifices young celebrities. Sports are an early version of the metaverse. We create scapegoats out of youthful, athletic, and uniquely talented humans among us and watch them imitate metaphorical wars, siphoning our primal urge for competition into these symbols rather than taking it out on each other. We pay millions and millions of dollars for it, cheer when these celebrities defeat our opponents, and condemn them when they make a misstep on the field or in their personal lives. As we evolve, we sanitize violence by letting others incarnate our instincts for us.

We haven't suspended human sacrifice as much as rebranded it.

Knowing this, on the one hand, there's a case to be made for virtual influencers like Lil Miquela. Perhaps if we're going to have celebrities and influencers and treat them as modern scapegoats, they ought to be completely fake, digital, and artificial.

When it comes to distinctly categorizing and identifying media's typology, it seems like Brud isn't just a collective of L.A. hipsters playing with the latest toys. There's a fair possibility they've thought long and hard about what they're architecting and its cultural implications, and have made several distinct choices as a result. For example, while Lil Miquela interacts with the real world, we're all aware she's a robot. We're all in on the game of kayfabe. If this is where the metaverse is going, if we're all in on the fun charade, and if that charade helps stir the fickle trends of popular culture, helps move some product off the shelves for a moment—then onward and upward! Out of all the roles and job descriptions designers and developers are racing to offload and automate, roles that have become a slog to our productivity and evolution, *please* let's offload the role of "celebrity" to the robots.

But I'd also be lying if I said I didn't have a gut feeling of caution when it comes to Lil Miquela and her creators.

People tend to create scapegoats when there's some underlying truth they don't want to admit.[4] That truth in our twenty-first-century culture is the fear of being ordinary. The myth that somehow our mere breath on earth is cheap, unsubstantial, or not enough makes it easy to both love and turn on those who appear "extra-ordinary." The crisis that is playing out on full display in the metaverse isn't a global plague or bloodshed, it's that we'll never live up to the superimposed, digitally enhanced versions of humanity we have crafted. So we band together and join the Great Distraction, "superhumanizing," then dehumanizing, the influencers we create, liking, canceling, celebrating, and sacrificing them on demand. We may even try to escape our ordinariness by hypercurating ourselves, branding our image and supersizing our shadow. It won't reconcile the fact that we, like Pinocchio trying to act his way into being real, or Peter Pan being unable to get his shadow to stick, are ordinary and finite apart from our projections, tethered to the ground once our batteries run out. Without a reverence for that ordinariness within us, we'll sacrifice our own selves, believing it will create the peace we long for.

Whether the influencers we create are real or virtual like Lil Miquela, they won't stop us from distracting ourselves from the inescapability of our shared ordinariness. Beyond that, the metaverse seems to be bringing about a change that could make these kinds of influencers even more of a threat to our sense of inner peace.

According to Girard, the reason scapegoats are often children, young women, or even animals among mythic cultures is because those attributes make them neutral objects. They have little to do with whatever conflict or crisis of difference is happening in the community. They're not actually part of the problem. The fact that they, in reality, have no skin in the game when it comes to whatever competition is unfolding makes it all the easier for the community to come together and blame them as an outside agitator. Some modern examples of this type of scapegoating include blaming immigrants for the loss of working-class jobs or discriminating against Asians during the global coronavirus outbreak. When a community can't solve the scarcity problem among them, they often conveniently cast blame on an otherwise neutral third party, no matter how myopic or false that blame is.

While all this continues to play out in the twenty-first century, when it comes to our twenty-four-seven hyperconnected media-verse, we stand, I believe, at a unique divergence from Girard's theory, a sort of Mimetic Theory 2.0.

When discussing the types of people we historically mimic, Girard talks a lot about "external mediators," those we desire and admire from afar. External mediators are a culture's royalty and elite—heroes and models to which most common people historically haven't had direct access—thus the reason they're called "external." But who would we consider "royalty" today? Are they not our celebrities, influencers—the personal brands we follow and admire?

Our modern scapegoats are no longer neutral. Before we discard them, they're what we aspire to.

Not only that—for the first time in human history, these influencers, or external mediators as Girard called them, are not so external. Far from our heroes being *in*accessible, we can now interact with them through our own pocket portals and platforms anytime we desire. They're encroaching their way into our lives. They are in our living rooms, our cars, and the palms of our hands!

We truly are, as Jeff Gomez mentioned in the previous chapter, in the Baroque phase of our own cultural super-narrative. We're overlapping, doubling up, and contradicting ourselves.

This brings us back to Lil Miquela. How do these changes affect what we do with our artificial friend and those like her? As I said earlier, the glaringly good news is that we may now be entering a phase of our social evolution where we finally stop turning real-life human beings into scapegoats. We may be able to prevent the next JoJo Siwa, LeBron James, or Japanese idol from being sacrificed.

That's no small feat, but it's only part of the story. We're still stuck with the problem of our mimetic nature.

If a virtual, hypercurated idol becomes the symbol for our desire, if something 100 percent manufactured and artificial becomes who we revere and strive to mimic, we may be setting ourselves up for an unprecedented mass crisis of disorientation and discontent.

When it comes to virtual influencers, what myths are we still perpetuating? Are we setting an expectation our wonderfully unpolished mixtures of matter and spirit can't possibly live up to? Are we simply Barbie-fying the future? Will Lil Miquela ever have cellulite? Will she ever have to balance a budget? Will she ever be shut out of an opportunity she didn't have a hand in curating? Maybe, but I don't think it's likely.

Whether virtual influencers like Lil Miquela and her ilk prove to be anything more than a temporary trend is yet to be determined. However, the strategy of manipulating the human likeness so it reflects a cultural ideal is as old as media itself. Regardless of where future influencers sit on the spectrum of fakeness, if they are going to truly contribute to our culture's health and sustainability, they can't be idols we desire to emulate or scapegoats we dehumanize and destroy. They have to transcend both archetypes to become something more useful to our collective journey toward a rehumanized world: they need to become jesters. If they become the characters of the modern myths we tell, they should be fools and mockers in service to the ordinary, carrying the message of how meaningless many of our desires have become, how fluid the definition of beauty is, how absurd the pursuit of perfection can be, how eye-rollingly easy it is to automate fame and status, and how difficult it is to replicate the fleeting, speckled beauty of a real-life, ordinary moment.

One last thing struck me as particularly odd while deep in the caverns of my rabbit-hole expedition into the world of Lil Miquela and her parent company, Brud. It's hard to miss Brud's point of view when it comes to storytelling. Brud's apparent dedication to this idea is one I've often heard in conversations about the future of the internet and the metaverse, and is plastered all over their website. It's this rallying cry that stories and characters shouldn't be owned, but rather should be the collective property of fans, audiences, and communities.

Here's a snippet from their homepage:

> We've reached a crossroads. Brud may have made virtual humans real—but you made them matter . . . You, the community of fans who've inspired us all along, have always been the most important part of this equation. But we're all stuck in [the current version of the web], where platforms exploit, platforms extract, and brands tell us all what to do . . . Stories don't live in a copyright document—they live in us.[5]

Yes! Now, everyone jump up on your prep-school desk chairs and recite "O Captain! My Captain!"

Forget any perceived pretense. Brud again has a point, a prophesy about the future of the internet I find genuinely exciting. It's why I think the concept of collective journey plays so nicely with idea of a metaverse we all collaboratively design. In our transmedia culture, where technology allows people to actively participate in stories, the collective h.. a chance to bec me more valuable than the individual. . es must be agreed upon. Ownership must be shared. Demo cy must win out over the Robot Muse. We are at onて ひ suming collective journey stories and living them

But if B. d is just as excited about this democratic shift, this fan-first mentality, it begs the question of why this $125 million company seems to have a business model centered around massive partnerships with major corporate and zeit-geist dictators like Prada and PacSun.

Are they only telling us what we *want* to hear? That's not collective journey, that's just kayfabe 3.0.

In Brud's defense, if its creators' words are any indication, the company seems aware that there is an apparent conflict here, and that debating such things is part of their whole strategy. Right now, I'm writing about Lil Miquela. You might have put down this book, picked up your device, and looked her up. Having the conversation about what all this means is the meta-story they're creating; the long game they at least say they're willing to play.

There have been instances where Brud has experimented with expanding Miquela's range past a consumer-brand novelty to an influencer who addresses matters of social justice and change, creating storylines that include her getting involved in racial-justice crusades or expressing same-sex attraction. These attempts have largely backfired.

Some things can't be manufactured. They're more effective when left to ordinary people.

10

IN DEFENSE OF GETTING LOST

Media as Gardening

ON A TOOTH THAT'S LOOSE

When you were new to the world it sprang up quickly and
   eagerly
Sharply biting at anything, everything.
Now it bows nearly 90 degrees
Almost humbled,
Its roots making your smile sore.

How easy it would be to take a piece of string and wrap it
   around,
Fasten it to a door
And let a moment of pain abolish it all.

But you tell me it's not time yet
That sometimes it takes very long for old things to leave
A hollow valley for a less brittle bone
Until what lies patiently inside you can reach the surface.

Beatitude
08.

BLESSED ARE THOSE WHO PLANT DIGITAL GARDENS, FOR THEY SHALL REAP WHAT THEY SOW.

Be like the fox who makes more tracks
than necessary, some in the wrong
direction. Practice resurrection.

—Wendell Berry

I didn't understand. I was consulting a friend on a new venture. The goal was to make schools more human centered. He kept saying he wanted his website to feel more like a labyrinth, a place where people could "get lost."

"It doesn't really work that way," I would say. "In fact, that's pretty much the opposite of what you want people to do when they visit your website."

People are supposed to navigate through a site quickly and easily, I thought. Everything should be designed strategically to get people to respond to a call to action, to make whatever decision you want them to in the smallest amount of time possible with the fewest steps.

He kept bringing up words and phrases like "trellis" and "meander" and "deep dive." Such thinking came naturally to him. To me it sounded like chaos. After all, he was an educator with a passion for changing the way we learn. I, on the other hand, had only recently left my manicured subdivision with its omniscient HOA. My thinking was still templated, manufactured, orderly, more like AstroTurf than wildflowers.

After about the third round of back-and-forth discussions with me gently pushing back against his wild notions of a digital space where potential customers could "get lost," he sent me an essay by a designer named Maggie Appleton called "A Brief History & Ethos of the Digital Garden."[1]

In it, she casts a vision for a different kind of internet, one that truly resembles the labyrinth my friend was imagining. She invited people to view the internet landscape as a garden—less of a collection of hypercurated individual brands and more of a rolling landscape tended and nurtured by farmers who cultivated paths for people to choose their own adventure. We've seen this kind of topography before, in the architecture of wiki networks and personal home pages built before the invention of what we now call blogging.

Appleton argues that the advent of templating software in the early 2000s, specifically Moveable Type, eventually gave way to blog templates like WordPress and Squarespace. Among other factors, this shift contributed to a more streamlined and homogenous internet. To me, this transition serves as yet another artifact, a historical turning point where a medium began dictating the message. It turned the web from a landscape guarded by coders (early digital farmers and craftspeople with knowledge of how to build) into a place where more individuals could plant their flag without such knowledge and care. The barrier to entry was lowered significantly.

Now, anyone, whether they were practicing creativity or not, could present the *appearance* of creativity simply by following a template. Thus began the great template-ization of things. Essentially, it turned the internet from a co-op gardening society to an individual industrial one. Where people once organically seeded new ideas, coding and cultivating ecosystems in community, others began performing and manufacturing micro-iterations of the same pattern. Items became cheaper and more streamlined to allow for mass production. Manual practices became automated, templatized, and homogenous. Linguistically, "creative expression" was downgraded to "content." Words became pictures, which became emojis.

As the influence and popularity of the internet grew and its governing powers (e.g., Google) became stronger, marketers discovered that call-to-action buttons should go here instead of there; that orange was the color clicked on most; that content should be organized this way instead of that way in order to be truly optimized; a photo should be cropped like so; one needs to do such-and-such for thoughts and opinions to be shared and "liked"; and so on.

You can see the downward spiral from organic to homogenized.

Talk about a mimetic crisis.

Back to Maggie and her essay. She urges us to consider what we produce on the web less as a performance and more like the practice of "learning in public." The metaphor she uses is that of tending a community garden—growing, pruning, curating, and experimenting with new ideas, harvesting the good ones and sharing the bounty, iterating on the bad ones without scuttling them out of embarrassment, all while constantly cross-pollinating, connecting ideas with each other through hyperlinks and hat tips. Writing to an audience immersed in hero's-journey thinking, she was quick to point out the now foreign nature of such an appeal:

> This isn't how we usually think about writing on the web. Over the last decade, we've moved away from casual live journal [*sic*] entries and formalised our writing into *articles* and *essays*. These are carefully crafted, edited, revised, and published with a timestamp. When it's done, it's done. We act like tiny magazines, sending our writing off to the printer. This is odd considering editability is one of the main selling points of the web. Gardens lean into this—there is no "final version" on a garden. What you publish is always open to revision and expansion."[2]

The mere act of reading Maggie's article, created on her own digital garden, sent me off wandering through a number of branching hyperlinks. I was "getting lost." Not only was it enlightening; I realized, for the first time in a long time, I was having fun on the internet! Not the passive, "scrolling and occasionally chuckling at cat videos" kind of fun. This was active, hippocampus-stimulating, contemplative fun, the kind one might feel exploring in the woods and being surprised by a stream or a wild buck in the distance.

Since the metaverse shows no sign of slowing its growth, I wonder if Maggie's essay isn't a directive for how we should instruct a generation to populate it.

The farmer-poet-activist Wendell Berry's words start to ring:

> Odd as I am sure it will appear to some, I can think of no better form of personal involvement in the cure of the environment than that of gardening. A person who is growing a garden, if he is growing it organically, is improving a piece of the world. He is producing something to eat, which makes him somewhat independent of the grocery business, but he is also enlarging, for himself, the meaning of food and the pleasure of eating. The food he grows will be fresher, more nutritious, less contaminated by poisons and preservatives and dyes than what he can buy at a store. He is reducing the trash problem; a garden is not a disposable container, and it will digest and re-use its own wastes. If he enjoys working in his garden, then he is less dependent on an

automobile or a merchant for his pleasure. He is involving himself directly in the work of feeding people.[3]

Sure, Mr. Berry is talking about the physical act of gardening. I hesitate to even quote him here in a book about media, technology, and the metaverse, as his works suggest he lives a lifestyle that has intentionally avoided all three of these subjects from encroaching on his life. Reading Wendell Berry, one might be convinced the best way to navigate the sweeping changes of the twenty-first century is to raise a barn, buy some sheep, and be done with it.

Forgive me, then, for removing the original context, but couldn't his suggestion about gardening apply to our contaminated and overrun digital landscape as well?

What we all love about gardens, whether they yield produce or pixels, is their penchant for iteration. Looking at the web through the lens of a digital garden, instead of a wrestling ring for kayfabe, invites us to iterate our thoughts in concert with other ordinary human beings around the planet. One rarely plants a few seeds and has a garden spring up perfectly on their first try. It's a constant dance between sunlight, soil, conniving varmints, and the chance of rain.

This shared boundedness is a much different approach than, say, the five-star grading system we now use to judge everything on the internet, products and people alike. If you're looking for an example of an industrialized internet, look no further. It's forced us all into a shallow and myopic template we now consult for everything, no matter how subjective the good or service may be. Dostoevsky's *The Brothers Karamazov* and Hugo's *Les Miserables*, both centuries-old literary masterpieces that took years to craft, hover around the low fours on Goodreads, the popular book-rating site owned by Amazon, a similar grade to *JoJo Siwa's Guide to the Sweet Life* which comes in at 4.27 stars. One of the most ironic aspects of Goodreads is that you can rate a book on the five-star scale without ever actually having to *write* anything to back up your review.

A friend of mine who owns a restaurant told me that upon opening, he invited a bunch of online critics and influencers to dine together one evening for free. One diner kept insisting my friend give him his watchband, which he'd been eyeing and coveting throughout the meal. His requests became more entitled as the night went on, growing from hinting to prying to uncomfortably pleading. His subtext was unmissable. Stars were being held for ransom.

The fact that the world's dominant internet companies insist on making this grading system inescapable for everyone from small business owners and restaurateurs to teachers and even artists demands that we bring a greater imagination to the metaverse. The future could be full of ordinary people liberated by technology or avatars shackled by scarlet letters. The choice is ours.

One simple and practical reform would be for major players like Google, Yelp, and Amazon to keep their user review capabilities, but discard the five-star component, if only for more subjective categories (sometimes snake oil deserves half a star). Instead, they could continue funneling users into writing, expressing, and cultivating their ideas with more intricate, qualitative language—promoting the propagation of thoughtful expression over mere content.

Think about the ramifications. It would force everyone to write (and read) not just register, to process their experiences and potentially arrive at more nuanced conclusions, as writing and reading have a habit of doing. Maybe then everyone with the newfound ability to become a critic may actually start to think critically. Instead of responding to others' hard work with the flip of a finger, perhaps people should consider putting in the effort of using all ten.

Who knows? Through the process of iteration, contemplation, pruning, and editing, we may find ourselves arriving at a different conclusion than the one we thought we would. That's what gardening is all about. A good gardener doesn't tell a seed how to grow; she creates the right conditions for it to branch how it was uniquely meant to.

To imagine the expanding metaverse as a garden is to imagine a place where our collective journey sees us all planting and nurturing ideas together without fear of being seen as frauds, and instead adopting the spirit of a farmer. It's a bold decision to stand in the middle of what's become a minefield and exclaim our ordinariness out loud, revel in our lack of expertise, and delight whenever we discover we were wrong about something, then rush to share in the bounty of those insights rather than weeding out our past mistakes.

In fact, some farmers will tell you it's actually beneficial to *keep* certain weeds in your garden. Some have a way of warding off bugs who are interested in devouring your harvest.

The idea of creating, iterating, liberating, and, perhaps most importantly, exposing that kind of process openly with others rather than deleting or burying it can seem like a vulnerable leap, but it's the kind of communal adventure that carries with it the power to till and establish the twenty-first-century landscape we actually hope for.

To do that, we first have to break the template.

In a digital garden we are creators, explorers, shepherds, and stewards.

In the current landscape we are livestock staring at our feed.

Industrialization, automation, and technological templates can be wonderful tools, but only when they make something more cumbersome easier. It is not cumbersome to imagine. It's not monotonous to explore. These are the gifts of God for the people of God, the merciful harvest of being an ordinary human.

If we teach our children that imagination, iteration, and transformation are not only permissible—in fact, they are some of our highest values—rather than presenting them with a technological factory where everything said is presented as real ("crafted, edited, revised, and published with a timestamp"), we might help curb the slippery notion that people themselves are sums to be rated on a scale, subscriptions to be canceled, unable to be reformed or reconciled, incapable of learning, developing, and iterating.

The burden to prove this, dear reader, is on you and me, the literate and aged, the last of the digital immigrants, the ones who contributed to such an industrialized landscape in the first place, decided where to stab our flag, and allowed our next generation to inherit what we built.

Gardens are possible, but first the land needs clearing. Grab a shovel and some fresh seed. There is great work to do.

11

A DOVE WITH CLAWS

CYBORG CAPTAIN'S LOG

When we were humans
we'd quarrel around the kitchen table
and have to soak our cuts in cold water.
Plants would stab us if we plucked them.
Squirrels would gnaw at our Christmas decorations.
Cooking itself was a kind of monotony.
We'd stir in circles while our thoughts scattered
    everywhere
like peanut butter over bread.

When we were humans
it was always waiting:
in grocery lines, at traffic stops
between hospital corridors and underneath our clothes.
The length it would take to sit and grieve, for example,
was nothing compared to how long it took to love a thing.
Having to mash limbs with someone just to feel at home
was bureaucratic at best.

When we were humans
we never really saw each other,
only the light we could trap
which would bounce off everything,
literally everything
until we could no longer deny it:
the insistent incarnation of star matter
that must be dealt with one way or another.

Beatitude
09.

BLESSED ARE THOSE WHO RADICALIZE KINDNESS, FOR THEY SHALL BE THE HOPEMONGERS WE NEED.

We are still dueling.

We may not walk around with swords or pistols, ready to slay whoever dares sully our family's good name, but we are still dueling, wielding a different weapon in the name of defense and preservation.

Today, a verbal altercation will arise and instead of someone drawing a gun, they'll reach for another weapon. They'll dig into their pocket for a black, handheld metal object, one that shoots differently.

I've seen arguments where both parties are simultaneously cursing and filming each other on their smartphones, both equally convinced they've caught the other committing a grave and punishable offense.

Pretty soon viral videos like these will resemble some kind of twenty-first-century Western with every bystander's weapon drawn, every finger on the circular red trigger, everyone capturing their own points of view.

Media has always been a form of ammunition and self-defense, but only recently has that form of defense become available on demand to most of us. Both René Girard and Marshall McLuhan believed that underneath violence lies a quest for one's identity; that as people begin to lose a sense of who they are, they resort to brutality as a means for survival. This explains most acts of terrorism and war, but it also explains our instinct to weaponize the very objects that call our identity into question. As twenty-first-century citizens, media technology connects us more than ever in what McLuhan called "the global village," but if those connections are between characters, avatars, and other farces of our ordinary selves, we may find ourselves grasping for what we believe to be reality, doing whatever it takes to belong to some truth more concrete than a vapor.

Therefore, the motive for drawing one's rectangular weapon seems to be preserving the truth of the moment, sort of a just-in-time capsule. The challenge we often overlook is that there is often so much *to* overlook.

Though powerful in some ways, our weapon of choice, the two-dimensional camera, is still quite crude. While it has unprecedented ability to affect the masses once it shoots its shot, when it comes to what it's capable of capturing in the moment, it resembles more of a Revolutionary War musket than a high-tech weapon of mass destruction. We're confined to the specific frame we're viewing, unable to analyze anything outside it. We're equally constrained by whenever the camera began recording as well as when it ended, with no ability to know what happened before or after—which, as we know, is where we often find the most pertinent information.

The alternative is that we all quite literally become body cameras. It's not hard to imagine humans roaming the earth with virtual vision goggles that are also recording at all times. That may sound hyperbolic, but as the metaverse threatens to engulf ever more aspects of our lives, deciding whether to be recording ourselves and each other at all times is a tangible choice we'll eventually have to make, both individually and as a society. Corporations, for example, have already begun to instate employee monitoring technology as more white-collar workers have started working remotely during the coronavirus pandemic. The age of constant capture is officially upon us.

To be clear, there are marginalized groups of people for whom that kind of instantaneous capture, the ability to whip out a just-in-time media musket, may be their only resort because de-escalation is not an option and gathering evidence or providing a last will and testament is all they can do in a life-threatening situation.

In 2016, for example, Diamond Reynolds quickly began documenting the aftermath of her boyfriend Philando Castile's murder after a police officer pulled them over and proceeded to strike four bullets into him when he reached for his wallet while her young daughter watched from the backseat of their car. Darnella Frazier, the courageous teenager who recorded the murder of George Floyd, also comes easily to mind, along with numerous other examples where life and death hang in the balance, where a swiftly caught record may be the only chance at justice. Sometimes weapons are necessary to prevent evil from persisting. Sometimes there is no additional context needed, no alternate angle necessary to capture inhumanity red-handed.

However, even in some of the worthiest of circumstances, look at everything these powerful pieces of independent media gave birth to. The chain of events they were able to ignite is staggering, their kinetic impact worthy of awe.

Weapons of any kind are not benign. They deserve reverence and respect.

When the situation is *not* life-threatening, when it isn't a case of seeking out systemic justice but merely justice for our feelings, our brands and not our actual lives, we mock the power our weapons hold and those who must use them out of necessity. Just because something is instant doesn't mean it's innocuous. Convenience doesn't permit flippancy. If our law-enforcement system has taught us anything in the past several years, it's that anytime a weapon becomes the first knee-jerk response, bypassing other tactics that might de-escalate the situation, it becomes a crutch and a cancer. No one wins.

Our micro-cameras might serve as self-defense weapons, but they do a poor job of de-escalating conflict. When we resort to our cameras as a weapon to hide behind, when we forget to see someone's hostility as a quest for identity and control and respond to them from that understanding, when we decide we're going to enhance the level of interference and noise, and place a barrier between us and them, we quite literally choose to see each other through a smaller lens.

As the poet Rainer Maria Rilke put it, "Perhaps everything that frightens us is, in its deepest essence, something helpless that wants our love."

That doesn't mean we let that gnarled mutation of love run us over or roam free without consequence. It means our most effective first response as fellow humans traversing a new century together may not always be to hold up a camera but instead hold up a mirror. It may mean choosing not to capture someone. It may mean first attempting to set them free.

As a media maker, I wrestle with all of this, the ways we choose to wield our weapons, the complexities they spawn—especially because I believe the camera and the microphone are some of the greatest tools we possess—not just to gather people but to reconcile them. Those kinds of stories, the ones that seem to last and have a genuine impact, are not instant. They're slow. They've been cradled by an imagination, refined again and again. The camera is the final touch, the last resort, a special effect on a three-dimensional truth worth bestowing.

When we choose to capture, edit, filter, reduce, cut, and manipulate our fellow species all in an instant, though, we create meta-conflicts in the metaverse. I believe there is another way we can wield the forces of media and technology to preserve ourselves besides dueling. Instead, we can do the hard, crawling work of listening, reflecting, de-escalating, and developing. These stories require a different kind of editing, a less self-preserving curation engrossed in snipping out biases and misunderstanding, adding in context, and incorporating multiple angles. That sounds less like social media and more like social work, the stuff of justice, reform, and reconciliation.

It sounds like a dove with claws.

That's a phrase Johnny Cash once used. It was the late 1960s and the country singer, whose toilet I once graced, found himself in a bit of a pickle. The Vietnam War was raging and the American troubadour was having trouble balancing his Southern, pro-military, patriotic personal brand with his increasing realization, along with most of the country, that this conflict was senseless, killing Americans who didn't have to die, and it needed to end. Would he continue the kayfabe, projecting one story publicly while inwardly believing another?

In a soul-searching pilgrimage, he packed his bags and traveled to Vietnam to sing to the troops. Not only did he sing, he slept among them, ate among them. Like them, he heard the sounds of bombs and people dying in the distance.

While there, a reporter approached Cash and asked, "Johnny, why are you here? Are you a dove? Or are you a hawk?"

During that time, those who considered themselves to be pro-peace coined themselves "doves," while those who were for the war were known as hawks. Here's how Johnny responded to the question of whether singing for the troops made him one or the other:

> Somebody said, "That makes you a hawk, doesn't it?"
>
> No, no that don't make me a hawk. But I said if you watch the helicopters bring in the wounded boys, and then you go into the wards and sing for 'em and try and do your best to cheer 'em up, so they can come back home, it might make you a dove with claws.[1]

Cash's answer was a poetic, non-dualistic image that for me conjures the likes of Christ, Martin Luther King Jr., and St. Nicholas (not the kayfabe version of Santa, but the real Greek who is known to have dropped gold coins through a father's window anonymously by night to save his daughters from slavery and stood in the way of a sword to protect three innocent men from execution). "A dove with claws" is a metaphor for the kind of tough, gritty, unrelenting kindness we need to navigate a future that would rather keep us dueling.

Notice that Cash's statement doesn't exclude the fight in him. So many of our conversations today around kindness and empathy are really more concerned with niceness (a banal, neutral, face-saving stand-in for kindness), as if that primal, evolutionary instinct we possess to conquer something, to overcome an object in our way, simply isn't there anymore, that it has somehow evaporated. Sometimes I think it's an easier jump to believe ourselves to be digital avatars floating around a disembodied metaverse because remembering that we're physical beings with ancestors, products of pain with smoke and fire in our lungs, urges and conflicting emotions in our bones, is far more difficult.

Yes, we've moved on from needing to constantly re-enact the tired, ancient hero's journey. No, we no longer need to scapegoat each other in sacrifice to the gods. What, then, do we do with our instinct to overcome?

The answer is not to keep dueling with each other. Nor is it to deny the ancient battle cry entangled in our humanity. Instead of ignoring some of our most human instincts or indulging them in dehumanizing conflicts, perhaps they need a new Everest to climb. Perhaps our evolution looks like doves with claws.

Do you want to win a war in the age of the metaverse? Win the war of intimacy. Fight to know the fellow members of your species, those whose ordinary presence justifies their kinship with you. Fight also to be known by them. Conjure up the courage to tell them how you feel, and have the discipline to listen long and hard enough when others do the same. That's the battle of the twenty-first century, the war of the worlds infiltrated by augmented filters and cold-blooded algorithms.

What if our greatest invitation, our most imperative directive for this unprecedented time when we find ourselves on the brink of singularity with media and technology, was to help the next generation navigate it by becoming radically kind, fierce creatures, by becoming doves with claws? Then we might succeed at liberating our *true* identities—our ordinary, primal, vulnerable, clay selves—to the same degree that we've liberated our hollow, translucent brands.

That may seem like an insurmountable battle at a time in history when the word "true" has become a cliché. Good, ordinary humans have scaled much bigger problems in the past. Let the improbability overwhelm you. Sit in the discomfort of knowing there is still more work to do, that there are still corners of our humanity left after so much has been automated. We found fire, chiseled the wheel, resurrected David by carving him from his gravestone, scaled our stories, and pressed them into the souls of people everywhere. Now, we must fight to ground each other in the same soil that started everything, the only stuff that will continue to sustain us even if we wish to abandon it for pixels and noise. We must battle against our own apathy, our own tendency toward automation, to see the ordinary miracle in a flesh-and-blood fellow who might just as well parade as our enemy in the virtual realm.

Yes, in a culture built around kayfabe, we're a bunch of Pontius Pilates exhaustedly asking, "What is truth?" And while we are indeed experiencing what feels like perhaps the most intense era of that crisis, it is also strangely comforting to concede that we are part of a long ancestry of remixes to an age-old song.

Shortly after Johnny Cash announced that he might be a "dove with claws," he was invited to perform at a concert for President Nixon at the White House. There Cash retold the story about him and the reporter. He then began to strum the chords to a new song he had just written, a gutsy one considering his audience, one that touched on the needless deaths associated with war, the incongruity of that fact with "the golden rule" America claims to value, all wrapped in a simple question, the song's title: "What Is Truth?"

Don't miss it. Don't miss the chosen medium and its message. Cash took a moment in history when everyone was questioning what truth was…and wrote a poem.

What does a dove with claws looks like? It looks like a poet, someone who can help us connect with the physicality of the earth we inhabit, awakening our senses and reorienting our emotions while pushing us to question, doubt, wrestle—in a word, fight.

Throughout history, poets have brought meaning, hope, order, and a reminder of soulfulness to any culture to which they've belonged. They've always been the ones responsible for ensuring that their culture doesn't dissolve into a mass of drones, compliant and controllable at the hands of an enemy. Even if a culture succumbed to captivity, it was the poet who worked to keep the flame of that culture alive, secured deep in the hearts of the community, in the imaginations of their children.

The necessary next step for a culture of digital natives and immigrants is to raise a generation of digital poets and prophets—those who have mastered the skills of empathy and imagination to express something eloquently, courageously, and truthfully. If hoping for a future without a metaverse is to live in denial, then perhaps we ought to get to work deciding what we *should* use it for before others decide it for us. How about gardens that cultivate empathy, sending us back to the real world as wiser, more integrated members of a sacred species? What about cathedrals offering space to meditate on the collective stories we tell, ones crafted slowly, shot from multiple angles, with enough time to uncover what we often overlook?

Before we can do that, we need to commission their builders. We must raise a generation of kayfabe-battling digital poets who write on a collective-journey canvas, doves with claws carrying an olive branch in the shape of whatever media tool they've mastered.

Looking out at the horizon, where the twenty-first century meets the twenty-second, I see hope. As machines offer to take over the lion's share of both our work and free time, as we're persuaded to spend more of our waking hours in the metaverse, there will come an eventual tipping point. Poets, those skilled in the once forgotten art of being ordinary, who can remind us of our humanity and the attributes that separate us from machines, will be in extremely high demand. Institutions from governments and classrooms to cubicles and factory floors will need experts trained to help us propagate peace, maintain physical and mental balance, exercise empathy, and resolve our duels. Before the twenty-first century, these services were viewed as ancillary amenities, even luxuries. But if the events that mark the turn of a new millennium—hyperpolitical polarization, worker burnout, or the rise of suicide and self-harm—are indicators of what's to come, the clock is ticking faster than ever before.

Unfortunately, without intentional leadership and education, without the urgent and vocal intervention of us, the digital elders of our culture, it's easy to imagine how this can all mudslide into another inequitable data point. Only the highest earners would be able to afford the kind of contemplative, mindful recalibration required to thrive in the twenty-first century, with their children being the only ones able to access the kind of learning necessary to think conceptually, critically, and empathetically, thus gaining a competitive edge.

The good news is that the overwhelming need for reforms to the issues just mentioned means the age of the digital poet is now upon us. Former prophets will now become practitioners. It will take systems listening to them, investing in them, and collaborating with them on wide-scale solutions *now* to ensure their work has enough time and bandwidth to reach everyone in society, including the most vulnerable, if not for moral reasons, then at least for the sake of our collective sustainability. More than that, it will take a populace of ordinary people like you and me redirecting our value to different places than where we've invested it.

Instead of overemphasizing the value of virality as we've come to understand it in the age of the Great Distraction, we ought to ask each other, "What kind of virality do we really hope for?"

So far, the metaverse has persuaded us to fixate on transient virality, the kind whose spread is rapid and linear, often feeding off others to become more powerful, but then vanishing almost as quickly as it erupted.

What I've become more interested in is *generational* virality, the kind of influence that spirals upward and outward over years, the stuff of slow stories crafted by fiercely kind fablers.

The paradox of this kind of influence is that it is often done on the margins, away from the spotlight, at a local level with very little immediate payoff. Generational virality spreads in such a way that it can remain dormant for years, doing some of its most impactful work just underneath the surface.

The obvious benefit of generational virality is that it's more sustainable and influential than transient virality. Prolific and self-replicating like a blackberry or ivy plant, generational virality is often generated while we simply inhabit our ordinary bodies, touch the common ground, and inhale the infinite sky.

With generational virality comes a paradox of anonymity. While this type of virality may not do much to boost one's digital expression or avatar in the metaverse, the work is still often vulnerable and exposing. And while it may not yield immediate followers, it often produces lasting leaders.

What's consistent is the genuine transformation it yields in a people over time, slowly and methodically bending back the crooked course of history so that, one by one, people remember the cavern they came from and the cavern where they'll rest, accept the unexchangeable, nonfungible gift of their ordinary incarnation, and run, full of breath in their lungs and blood in their heart, to tell the others where the fire can be found.

THE BEATITUDES OF MEDIA TECHNOLOGY

Blessed are those who consider humanity's relationship with media as urgent a crisis as its relationship to climate, for they shall correct our fatal course.

Blessed are those who long for a fireplace more than a jetpack, for they shall revitalize the American Dream.

Blessed are those who urge media to bend toward democracy, for they shall prevent the opposite.

Blessed are those who help distinguish truth from fiction, for they shall be called artists.

Blessed are those who huddle close, for they shall be set free.

Blessed are those who tell new stories, for they shall be called peacemakers of the twenty-first century.

Blessed are those who let go of old myths in the metaverse, for they shall find new meaning in the real world.

Blessed are those who plant digital gardens, for they shall reap what they sow.

Blessed are those who radicalize kindness, for they shall be the hopemongers we need.

ACKNOWLEDGMENTS

This book would not have been possible without Matt Holt's investment or Katie Dickman's editing talent, both of which I consider invaluable.

I'm also grateful to Jeff Gomez, who generously shared his ideas on the collective journey for this project and pushed me out of my cynicism into a perspective of hope, proving to me that he incarnates what he teaches.

As a kid, even though I grew up in the eighties and nineties, I wasn't allowed to watch professional wrestling. I first heard the term "kayfabe" during my time in Nashville from fellow writers David Dark and Greg Thornberry. They've both done a remarkable job of unpacking how it plays out, specifically when it comes to our political climate. I encourage you to read both of their work. In addition, several conversations with my good friend Dr. Marc Mednick helped shape sections of chapter VI, where the concept of kayfabe is first explored.

I'd also like to acknowledge Nic McKinley, whom *VICE* once called "the real Jack Ryan." He gave me the definition of humility you've read in chapter II and also made me realize the etymology of the word "disintegrate," which I use a few times throughout the book. A former CIA operative, Nic started an organization that fights the injustice of human trafficking. It's called DeliverFund and it's worth your attention.

Since I first discovered the work of Marshall McLuhan more than a decade ago, I've been under its spell. You can imagine my surprise when his grandson, Andrew, the director of the McLuhan Institute, responded to my random request to connect. Even more surprised was I to find both a kindred spirit and a friend. I'm so grateful for his guidance and contribution to this project.

Last, Kelly, who takes up more than half of my soul, gets the credit for anything else you find remotely interesting in this book. In addition to her numerous ideas and contributions that have made their way throughout these pages, she's not only been a steadfast sounding board and collaborator, but also has generously given me the time to contemplate, write, and edit this project in the midst of raising a full family during a year when we decided to move from one state to another. For these and countless other reasons that could fill their own volume, I am blissfully in debt for the remainder.

NOTES

01. Branding Is for Cows. Belonging Is for People.

1   Taylor Holland, "What Is Branding? A Brief History," Skyword, August 11, 2017, https://www.skyword.com/contentstandard/branding-brief-history/#:~:text=Brand%20originally%20referred%20to%20a,much%20older%20than%20the%20word.

2   Jenny Odell, *How to Do Nothing: Resisting the Attention Economy* (New York: Melville House, 2019).

02. Bearing Witness

1   Matthew 5:5 and 5:7, English Standard Version.

03. The Ghost of John Hill: Media as a Crisis Discipline

1   "Tobacco Tactics: Hill & Knowlton," University of Bath, May 22, 2018, https://tobaccotactics.org/wiki/hill-knowlton/.

2   Kelly D. Brownell and Kenneth E. Warner, "The Perils of Ignoring History: Big Tobacco Played Dirty and Millions Died. How Similar Is Big Food?" *The Milbank Quarterly* 87, no. 1 (2009): 259–94. https://doi.org/10.1111/j.1468-0009.2009.00555.x.

3   US Surgeon General, *Protecting Youth Mental Health*, 2021, https://www.hhs.gov/sites/default/files/surgeon-general-youth-mental-health-advisory.pdf.

4   "Facebook Whistleblower Frances Haugen: The 60 Minutes Interview," CBS News, October 3, 2021, https://www.cbsnews.com/video/facebook-whistleblower-frances-haugen-misinformation-public-60-minutes-video-2021-10-03/.

5   Chris Ciaccia, "Former Facebook Exec Won't Let Own Kids Use Social Media, Says It's 'Destroying How Society Works,'" *FOX News,* December 12, 2017, https://www.foxnews.com/tech/former

-facebook-exec-wont-let-own-kids-use-social-media-says-its
-destroying-how-society-works.

6   Scott Pelley, "Whistleblower: Facebook Is Misleading the Public
on Progress Against Hate Speech, Violence, Misinformation,"
60 Minutes, October 4, 2021, https://www.cbsnews.com/news/
facebook-whistleblower-frances-haugen-misinformation-public
-60-minutes-2021-10-03/.

7   Marshall McLuhan, *Understanding Media: The Extensions of Man*
(New York: McGraw-Hill, 1964).

8   Joseph B. Bak-Coleman, Mark Alfano, Wolfram Barfuss, et al.,
"Stewardship of Global Collective Behavior," *PNAS* 118, no. 27
(2021), https://www.pnas.org/doi/10.1073/pnas.2025764118.

9   Andrew McLuhan, "Macro Media Literacy," *Medium,* April 29,
2021, https://medium.com/@andrewmcluhan/macro-media-literacy
-f6352e085c3a.

10   Ibid.

11   Tristan Harris and Aza Raskin, "A Conversation with Facebook
Whistleblower Frances Haugen [transcript]," *Your Undivided
Attention* (podcast), Center for Humane Technology, October 18,
2021, https://assets-global.website-files.com/5f0e1294f002b1bb26e
1f304/616e2fde127454ff56485415_CHT%20Undivided%20
Attention%20Ep42%20Facebook%20Whistleblower%20Frances
%20Haugen%20in%20Conversation.pdf.

04. The Revolution Will Not Be Streamed: Media and the American Dream

1   Joseph McBride, *Frank Capra: The Catastrophe of Success*
(Jackson: University Press of Mississippi, 2011).

2   Will Chen, "FBI Considered *It's a Wonderful Life* Communist
Propaganda," *WiseBread*, December 24, 2006, https://www
.wisebread.com/fbi-considered-its-a-wonderful-life-communist
-propaganda.

3   Christopher Wilson, "What 'It's a Wonderful Life' Teaches Us
About American History," *Smithsonian Magazine,* December 16,
2021, https://www.smithsonianmag.com/smithsonian-institution
/what-its-a-wonderful-life-teaches-us-about-american-history
-180979223/.

4   Abigail Haworth, "Why Have Young People in Japan Stopped
Having Sex?," *The Guardian*, October 20, 2013, https://www

.theguardian.com/world/2013/oct/20/young-people-japan-stopped
-having-sex.

5   "Young People Losing Interest in Sex, but Why?," *Kuchikomi*
(blog), *Japan Today,* August 24, 2020, https://japantoday.com
/category/features/kuchikomi/young-people-losing-interest-in-sex
-but-why.

6   Marnie Hunter, "The World's Happiest Countries for 2022," CNN,
March 18, 2022, https://www.cnn.com/travel/article/worlds-happiest
-countries-2022-wellness/index.html.

7   Anna Altman, "The Year of Hygge, the Danish Obsession with
Getting Cozy," *The New Yorker,* December 18, 2016, https://www
.newyorker.com/culture/culture-desk/the-year-of-hygge-the-danish
-obsession-with-getting-cozy.

05. Senator Cruz and the Robot Muse: Media as Public Space

1   Ariana Garcia, "Ted Cruz Caught Checking Twitter Mentions After
Yelling at SCOTUS Hearing," *Chron,* March 24, 2022, https://
www.chron.com/politics/article/Ted-Cruz-Twitter-checks-phone
-Ketanji-Brown-17025661.php.

2   Thomas W. Hazlett, David Porter, and Vernon Smith, "Radio Spectrum
and the Disruptive Clarity of Ronald Coase," *Journal of Law &
Economics* 54, no. 4 (2011): S125–65, https://doi.org/10.1086/662992.

3   Robert D. Hershey Jr., "F.C.C. Votes Down Fairness Doctrine in a
4–0 Decision," *New York Times,* August 5, 1987, http://www
.nytimes.com/1987/08/05/arts/fcc-votes-down-fairness-doctrine-in
-a-4-0-decision.html.

4   Nicholas Carr, *The Shallows: What the Internet Is Doing to Our
Brains* (New York: W. W. Norton, 2010).

5   Ibid.

6   Stanford University, "Tracking 18th-Century 'Social Network'
Through Letters," YouTube video, December 14, 2009, 2:28,
https://www.youtube.com/watch?v=nw0oS-AOIPE.

7   Lyndon Baines Johnson, "President Johnson's Remarks,"
Corporation for Public Broadcasting, November 7, 1967, https://
cpb.org/aboutpb/act/remarks.

8   Kat Tenbarge (@kattenbarge), "For people who have been
studying the misinformation campaign around the Depp v Heard
trial, this verdict is chilling. The success of Depp's 'redemption

arc' narrative reveals a lot about our social media platforms and ourselves. A thread of things I learned during Depp v Heard:," Twitter, June 1, 2022, https://mobile.twitter.com/kattenbarge/status /1532115409889026048.

9   David Folkenflick, "You Literally Can't Believe the Facts Tucker Carlson Tells You. So Say Fox's Lawyers," *NPR,* September 29, 2020, https://www.npr.org/2020/09/29/917747123/you-literally -cant-believe-the-facts-tucker-carlson-tells-you-so-say-fox-s-lawye.

06. Wrestling Killed the Reality Star: Media as Kayfabe

1   David Dark, "On Metaphor and Kayfabe," *Dark Matter* (Substack), May 3, 2021, https://daviddark.substack.com/p/on-metaphor-and -kayfabe.

2   Wikipedia, s.v. "*An American Family*," last modified February 2, 2023, https://en.wikipedia.org/wiki/An_American_Family.

3   Ian Sample, "Social Media May Affect Girls' Mental Health Earlier Than Boys', Study Finds," *The Guardian,* March 28, 2022, https://www.theguardian.com/science/2022/mar/28/social-media -may-affect-girls-mental-health-earlier-than-boys-study-finds.

4   Jason M. Nagata, Kyle T. Ganson, Puja Iyer, et al., "Sociodemographic Correlates of Contemporary Screen Time Use Among 9- and 10-Year-Old Children," *Journal of Pediatrics* 240 (2021), https://www.jpeds.com/article/S0022-3476(21)00862-3 /pdf#:~:text=Boys%20reported%20higher%20overall%20 screen,all%20modalities%20except%20video%20chat.

5   Nilay Patel, "Is the Metaverse Going to Suck? A Conversation with Matthew Ball," *The Verge,* July 19, 2022, https://www.theverge.com /23269170/what-is-the-metaverse-matthew-ball-interview-decoder -podcast; Ledger Insights, "LEGO, Epic to Launch Kids Metaverse Experience," April 11, 2022, https://www.ledgerinsights.com/lego -epic-to-launch-kids-metaverse-experience/.

6   Steve Kovach, "Next for the Metaverse: Convincing You It's Not Just for Kids," *CNBC,* December 12, 2022, https://www.cnbc.com /2021/12/22/here-are-the-companies-building-the-metaverse-meta -roblox-epic.html.

7   Erron Kelly, "Making the Metaverse Safe," *GamesBeat,* November 4, 2022, https://venturebeat.com/games/making-the-metaverse-safe/.

8   Rachel Ehmke and Dave Anderson, "A Parent's Guide to Dealing with Fortnite: The Social Draw," Child Mind Institute, last updated October 12, 2021, https://childmind.org/article/parents-guide -dealing-fortnite/#the-social-draw.

9   Leslie Katz, "Gen-Z, You'll Have to Pry the 'Hostile' Thumbs-Up Emoji from My Old, Dead Hands," CNET, October 19, 2022, https://www.cnet.com/culture/internet/gen-z-youll-have-to-pry-the -hostile-thumbs-up-emoji-from-my-old-dead-hands/.

10   "Wynton Marsalis Moves Jazz to 'Higher Ground,'" NPR, September 2, 2008, https://www.npr.org/templates/story/story.php ?storyId=94198246

07. Temperance Town: Media in Moderation

1   "Odd Ohio: Heart of Temperance Movement Once Beat in Westerville," *Akron Beacon Journal,* August 13, 2016, https://www .beaconjournal.com/story/lifestyle/travel/2016/08/13/odd-ohio-heart -temperance-movement/10505028007/.

2   Ibid.

3   Ken Gordon, "Westerville's Evolution from 'Dry' to 'Wet' Now Being Celebrated," *Columbus Dispatch,* July 5, 2019, https://www .dispatch.com/story/news/local/2019/07/05/westerville-s-evolution -from-dry/4758886007/.

4   Ibid.

08. The Hero Is Dead: Media as Collective Journey

1   Brian Rafferty, "How the Guy Who Played Jar Jar Binks Survived the Fandom Menace," *Wired,* July 15, 2017, https://www.wired.com /2017/07/ahmed-best-jar-jar-binks-new-podcast.

2   You can read some of Jeff Gomez's pop culture insights on his blog, https://blog.collectivejourney.com.

09. What to Do with Lil Miquela: Media as Mythology

1   Nicole de Ayora bio, Brud website (archived), accessed February 13, 2023, https://web.archive.org/web/20220519044317/https:// www.brud.fyi/.

2   Richard Cocks, "Two Kinds of Sacrifice: René Girard's Analysis of Scapegoating," *Voegelin View,* April 9, 2020, https://voegelinview .com/two-kinds-of-sacrifice-rene-girards-analysis-of-scapegoating/.

3   Hoover Institution, "Insights with René Girard," YouTube video, December 7, 2009, 36:32, https://www.youtube.com/watch?v=BN kSBy5wWDk&t=1719s.

4   Luke Burgis, "The Ugly Psychology Behind Scapegoating," Big Think, YouTube video, November 14, 2021, 8:44, https://www .youtube.com/watch?v=cLa0zqShCcw&t=337s.

5   Brud website (archived), accessed February 13, 2023, https://web .archive.org/web/20220519044317/https://www.brud.fyi/.

10. In Defense of Getting Lost: Media as Gardening

1   Maggie Appleton, "A Brief History & Ethos of the Digital Garden," accessed January 5, 2023, https://maggieappleton.com /garden-history.

2   Ibid.

3   Wendell Berry, *Think Little: Essays* (Berkeley, CA: Counterpoint, 2019).

11. A Dove with Claws

1   Jonathan Silverman, "A 'Dove with Claws'? Johnny Cash as Radical," *Journal for the Study of Radicalism* 1, no. 2 (2007): 91–106, http://www.jstor.org/stable/41887579.

"Moderately gifted."

—One Very Reputable Online IQ Test

Photo by Jeffrey Joseph

CJ Casciotta is an author of questionable book titles, a poet, and a part-time puppeteer making his parents proud they decided to invest in private education.

As a creative strategist and media producer, CJ has partnered with notable brands like MGM Studios, Delta Airlines, Sesame Street, and Lululemon. He's also the creator of Ringbeller, an award-winning media and technology project helping kids learn urgent skills like creativity and kindness in schools around the world.

CJ travels globally speaking to creative professionals at venues like Creative Mornings, TEDx, and STORY. In addition, his work has been featured by *Forbes*, Salon, CBS, MTV, and TechCrunch, which are, like, big deals, right?

Most importantly, CJ is a husband and dad figuring out how to raise thoughtful, caring humans in the twenty-first century whenever he's not busy writing about himself in the third person.